PARTNERS WITH YOUTH

How Adults and Teen-Agers
Can Work Together

PARTNERS WITH YOUTH

How Adults and Teen-Agers Can Work Together

by

DOROTHY M. ROBERTS

ASSOCIATION PRESS
New York

PARTNERS WITH YOUTH
HOW ADULTS AND TEEN-AGERS CAN WORK TOGETHER

Copyright © 1956 by
National Board of Young Men's Christian Associations
Association Press, 291 Broadway, New York 7, N. Y.

Second printing, May, 1957

Library of Congress catalog card number: 56–10664

 475

Printed in the United States of America

ACKNOWLEDGMENTS

This book has been possible only through the co-operative interest of a great many people. Beyond those to whom appreciative credit is given in the text are many others whose help has been invaluable.

Deserving of special thanks are Elma Phillipson, Bernice Bridges, Violet Seider, Hester Ann Bradbury; Ruth Teichman and two members of her staff, Mrs. Nail Xenia and Eleanor Zolotow; Miriam Ephraim, Howard Gibbs, and Dr. Max Wolff, for conference time given in the early stages of the manuscript.

I am indebted also to Dr. Willis H. Griffin, Teachers College, Columbia University; to William J. Flynn, Assistant Director, Junior Red Cross; Warren Schmidt and Rollyn Winters, 4-H Clubs; to George B. Corwin and John A. Ledlie, National Council of YMCA's.

To the following young people I wish to express my gratitude: Nick Johnson, Mason Hendricks, Bob Potter, Dorothy Ann Sheets, Douglas Gray Saunders, Seldon M. Kruger, W. Peter Miller, Raphael Kosakoff, and Richard Rineer.

Special thanks are due to each member of the Wisconsin Youth Committee for Community Participation, especially to Alvin Lunde, its president in 1954-55, who unconsciously contributed much through his friendly teen-age letters; and to all my young friends in Hi-Y who helped me to check the accuracy of my point of view about teen-age ideas and feelings.

And last, but by no means least, much appreciation is due to Mrs. Donald Kimball and Miss Muriel Ford; and to my husband for his patience and understanding during the preparation of the manuscript.

DOROTHY M. ROBERTS

CONTENTS

PARTNERS WITH YOUTH

*How Adults and Teen-Agers
Can Work Together*

CHAPTER 1 | ADULT ATTITUDES TOWARD THE TEEN-AGE SITUATION

Adult partnership with youth is an ever-present possibility provided young people can feel that adults have genuine confidence in them. Many adults and teen-agers, as this book will give evidence, have already found that a partnership feeling can be real, and that it produces benefits to the community and satisfactions to themselves which they had not known were possible. There is a recognizable but still a limited trend toward the development of this kind of adult-adolescent relationship. But the majority in both age groups do not yet realize that such a relationship is possible, or, if they realize its possibility, they do not always know a way to achieve it.

Within this majority, many adults have had their normal degree of confidence in all teen-agers badly shaken by the long-extended emphasis on delinquency. The teen-age situation is viewed with alarm, and the discussion of it carries the implication that little is good about it. There is the further implication that teen-agers, by themselves, have created the problem situation, and that adults have had little or nothing to do with its development.

The first purpose of the analysis in this chapter is to enable adults to look at the situation more critically in order to see what relationship they may have to it; to see the teen-age group as a whole and in perspective; to determine the real problem in relation to teen-agers and to indicate the direction in which a solution lies.

The second purpose of this analysis is to provide a backdrop against which the need for adult confidence in teen-agers may be more clearly seen and against which the stories of adult-youth partnership development may be better evaluated as one significant answer to the so-called "teen-age problem."

Any analytical process consists of several steps: to state the problem as seen at present; to isolate known factors contributing to the problem; to discover new factors not previously recognized as contributing to the problem; either to confirm the original statement of the problem or to restate it more accurately. Once a problem is accurately defined, the direction in which a solution lies becomes clear.

The Analysis

We accept the premise that the teen-age situation is the problem. Our first known factors are (1) that delinquency exists and that it is a problem, and (2) that teen-agers are not isolated from adults. During their hours at home, in school and in church, during their travel on public conveyances, in the movies, and in many other diverse ways within the larger community, young people are constantly exposed to the attitudes of adults, both toward adult problems and toward teen-agers and their problems.

ATTITUDES ARE CONTAGIOUS

Individual attitudes toward problems and toward life in its essence exert a subtle but dynamic influence on others. Individual attitudes are cumulative and produce a total kind of effect. This total effect determines whether there is an atmosphere of reasonable, confident faith in life itself and in the belief that honest, intelligent effort will produce a solution to all problems, or whether there is an atmosphere of uncertainty and discouragement.

There seems to be a good deal of evidence that the negative atmosphere is the dominant one which, in turn, penetrates teen-age feeling about life, about themselves, and about adults. Grown-ups must depend upon youth to preserve and enhance their free and responsible way of life. Unless adults have confidence in their own ability to meet their own problems, boys and girls have no source of confidence upon which to draw, other than that which they can find in themselves. Unless what confidence adults have is based on inner spiritual security, there is difficulty in trusting others, including teen-agers. Unless adults can believe in the potentialities of boys and girls, they in turn feel insecure and have difficulty finding legitimate confidence in themselves and in older people upon whom they must still depend for guidance.

Finding spiritual security for themselves is the adults' own problem, but adult confidence in teen-agers is the birthright of youth. To demonstrate confidence in them is the responsibility of adults to them.

It is of the utmost importance to youth that adult attitudes toward them be fair and that perspectives about them be accurate; otherwise, they instinctively know that adults do not believe in them now or in their potentialities for the future. If they do not trust their parents, advisers, and older friends, the opportunity to help them is lost, and likewise adults have failed in responsibility to them.

And so, a look at the kinds of observable adult attitudes toward their own problems and toward teen-agers, as a sort of gauge to their own attitudes is in order at this point.

ADULT ATTITUDES TOWARD THEIR OWN PROBLEMS
AND TOWARD TEEN-AGERS

It should be made perfectly clear at the outset that this analysis of adult attitudes is in no way a scientific research project. It is based on conversations, observation, and the detailed reading of and thumbing through many books. These books, all of which have been published since 1950, are designed to strengthen adult confidence and to inspire spiritual fortitude.

Adult attitudes to the complex problems of our adult world appear to fall into several categories. Some are held by practical idealists with that inner spiritual security which makes them know that all adult problems can be solved *if* each one tries hard enough. There are those who are indifferent to world and social problems and do not give these matters much thought. There are some who feel that there are satisfactory answers to social problems somewhere but that an individual can do little or nothing to find them. Still others see only world delinquency. These are convinced that "there have always been wars and there always will be," that "there have always been bad people in the world and there always will be," and that nothing can be done about it.

The cumulative effect of these kinds of attitudes toward our social and world problems appears to be a dominating atmosphere of lack of confidence, indifference, and frustration. A generalized feeling of discouragement often projects itself into a specific problem situation and makes it also appear unsolvable. This seems to have happened in the case of teen-agers.

Those experts who are trying to find the causes of delinquency and a cure for it have voiced the opinion that this special problem is all of a piece with the over-all atmosphere of world tension and a reflection of adult personal and social problems which have not been courageously and intelligently met. They feel that this atmosphere of general tension is a contributing factor both to the brutality of much of the delinquent behavior and also to the teen-age restlessness which too often finds relief in vandalism.

The kinds of observable adult attitudes toward teen-agers seem to add up to about the same degree of indifference, discouragement, and frustration about them as about adult problems. There are some adults who know enough responsible teen-agers to have developed confidence in individuals and in the age group as a whole. Others may have confidence in a few individuals but feel discouraged about the rest of them. Still others are too busy with their own affairs to give any of them much thought. Many other adults feel that something should be done about the situation but they do not know where to start or what to do. Adults who are dealing only with delinquents are absorbed with their problems and with those which such destructive behavior creates for others. Such concentration on one segment of the total age group tends to blur the image of the whole, thus unintentionally adding to the feeling of discouragement about all of them.

There seems to be strong circumstantial evidence that the emphasis on delinquent teen-agers has done much toward creating adult attitudes of discouragement when trying to deal with them. There also seems to be much circumstantial evidence that this emphasis on delinquency and its resulting adult attitudes also affects teen-agers' attitudes toward themselves, toward other teen-agers, and toward adults.

THE EFFECT OF THE EMPHASIS ON DELINQUENCY UPON ADULT ATTITUDES TOWARD ALL TEEN-AGERS

During the two years that we have been trying to find out what adults and teen-agers can do and are doing co-operatively in organizations and communities, we have been making some informal checks of adult opinion about teen-agers. Here are a few typical experiences which resulted from our efforts.

1. A dozen or more women were relaxing in a department store lounge. A small child was having fun with the swinging door leading into the lounge. It was evident that all were disturbed lest the child be hurt by someone suddenly opening the door from the other side. Finally one woman said, "Where *is* that child's mother?" and got up to restrain the child. Immediately another said, "It's no wonder that teen-agers are such a dangerous bunch when mothers don't care what their children do."

Then and there a heated discussion followed about present-day adolescents. The general feeling was that they were all delinquent. The opinion was general that none of them should be allowed out after dark. Only one person in the group had any first-hand information about the many constructive activities of nondelinquents boys and girls. When some of this information was given one woman said, "I guess that's right, but . . ." No opinions were obviously changed, but perhaps a new chain of thoughts was forged. There is no way of knowing, because that identical group will never meet again.

2. We found that the subject of teen-agers rarely failed to come up in any adult group of friends or acquaintances. When it did, it was invariably opened with a groan of "Oh, those teen-agers!" The groan was always followed by a recount of the latest adolescent crimes with each person adding something. It was not at all unusual to have the conversation close with a remark somewhat like this: "Everything is in such a mess—there is just nothing an individual can do about anything." It rarely happened that more than one person denied this statement or was able to counteract the only information about teen-agers which such a group had available.

3. In a New York subway train a group of six or eight high school boys and girls boarded the train, laughing and talking among themselves. They were noisy, but their talk was about their own teen-age affairs and their language was in no way objectionable. Apart from the fact that to be as noisy as they were, was inconsiderate of other passengers, they were doing no harm at all. Looking around the car, there was nothing but disgust on the faces of the adult passengers with no evidence at all of good-natured adult tolerance of teen-age high spirits because school was out. One person was heard to remark to his neighbor, "I don't know what the world is coming to, the awful things teen-agers do these days."

4. In a club made up of twenty or so men in various professions one member presented a paper on juvenile delinquency. The tone of the paper created the impression that teen-agers were a hopeless lot and that the problem was too big for any of us. Out of the group there was only one man, a physician, who could speak up for the healthy, normal boys and girls. He could do so because he had two sons and a daughter in the YMCA Hi-Y program. He knew the number of boys and girls that were active in it and the constructive things many of them did which were an influence for good among the students in the high school and in the community.

5. In talking with parents of young children, we found that many of them are already jittery about what kind of teen-agers their children will become. They, too, seemed to be in-

formed only about the delinquents and seemed to fear that there was one lurking in every corner, ready to pounce on their child.

6. And finally—in a certain local organization there is an adult advisory committee for the youth program. Several teen-agers serve with the adults. One evening the discussion centered around how to interest parents in the program. One girl spoke up. She said, "The parents had just better get interested—look at how awful the teen-agers are! The papers are full of the dreadful things they do." One of the adults said, "Yes, the papers are full of that sort of thing, but you know that all teen-agers are not like that. We have four hundred of them right here in our program, and they don't do dreadful things." The girl flashed back, "Sure I know that, but our parents don't. They think we are like all the rest."

On the basis of these illustrations and many more like them it seems reasonable to say that the attitudes toward all teen-agers, shown by many adults of different backgrounds and interests, have been adversely affected by the emphasis on delinquency. These same adults seem to have little or no information about what nondelinquent boys and girls are doing.

THE ADVERSE EFFECT OF DELINQUENCY PUBLICITY ON TEEN-AGERS THEMSELVES

Conversations with many boys and girls lead to the observation that they react to the delinquency publicity with frustration, resentment, apparent indifference, and fear. Such feelings exist in varying degrees of intensity in individuals and reflect in their general and specific behavior, depending mostly upon the degree of maturity each has attained.

Teen-agers who show delinquent behavior have all these feelings in a marked degree. They do not understand their problems. Most often their experience with adults, from early childhood, leads them to believe that no adult can be depended upon. This is why adults who know how to reach out to them and are able to help them, have so much difficulty in gaining their confidence, without which no help is possible. These boys and girls are among the least mature, emotionally.

Others among the least mature group feel a restlessness which they do not understand. They are often bored. They are still too immature to have developed the inner resources to find constructive activity, unaided. Often they feel discouraged. The attitude of "What's the use?" too frequently leads them into mischief and vandalism of varying degrees of destructiveness.

Among those who show no delinquency tendencies at all, many appear indifferent to their age group reputation but reveal that they are inwardly resentful when gently drawn into talking about it. Others are more articulate and talk about their resentment freely. They all feel that something should be done to prove that they are not delinquent, but they don't know what to do. Large numbers of these apparently indifferent but actually resentful boys and girls have no adult sponsored youth group affiliation through which they might find the courage and the opportunity to relieve their feelings adequately and to gain support from adults who believe in them.

Many among the most mature boys and girls become rebellious and say, "We are sick of being lumped with the delinquent minority." These gladly accept the opportunity to "do something" which comes through their adult sponsored youth organization. These young people look upon adults as their allies and manage to find some who are ready and willing to help them tackle this or any other problem of concern to them. In action, with adult support, they maintain their self-respect and often strengthen the hands of less confident teen-agers in the organization and community.

Others, who are equally active in such organizations, but less mature, seek the security of a group of friends whom they know. They show fear of others in their own age group and tend to be suspicious of adults whom they do not know. These and other fearful boys and girls are the ones most apt to be deeply affected by their age group reputation. Fear and suspicion, without legitimate cause, are paralyzing emotions, especially for young people whose ideas and emotions are all in flux. They retard the maturing process and hold the young persons back from finding release in the kind of activity which the more mature ones seek and also find. After one or two experiences with their parents some of them say, "Gee, if I'm fifteen minutes late getting home my mother just stands and looks at me. I know she is thinking, 'I wonder if that boy of mine has gotten into trouble.' "

Others say, "Gee, if we laugh out loud on the street, or push another guy around, or have our arm around a girl, the grown-ups look at us with long faces. We know they are thinking, 'There goes another bunch of those delinquents.' It's awful!"

A big, husky, six-foot boy said, "I wouldn't walk alone after dark in Brooklyn or Harlem or downtown New York—you just run the risk of getting beat up."

A group of boys were talking with an adult. The subject of delinquency came up spontaneously. The adult asked, "What proportion of the boys and girls in your high school do you think are delinquent?" Without a moment's hesitation a boy said, "At least 35 per cent." The others agreed that the figure was about right. Figures were checked later. The fact was that in that particular school with 2700 students, less than 1 per cent actually got into serious trouble or committed acts of mild or serious vandalism.

The adult then posed this question: "How do you know when boys or girls are delinquent?" Another boy replied, "All you have to do is look at them, and besides they all hang together in their own crowd. All you have to do is get one of them alone, and he's yellow—scared he's going to get beat up himself." The others shook their heads in complete agreement. When the adult pointed out that it was characteristic of all teen-agers "to hang together in their own crowd" the spokesman looked thoughtful and then said, almost with relief, "Gee, that's right, I never thought of that."

The possibility of having a youth center was being discussed with a dozen or so of these boys and girls. Their reaction was, "It would only be a waste of money. All the tough guys would move in and the decent kids would move out." When asked, "Don't you think your decent behavior could set a standard and influence others?" their quick and almost unanimous response was, "Gosh, no—what could we do?"

There seems to be little doubt that both adults and teenagers are fully aware that delinquency exists, that their attitudes are affected by the fact and that teen-agers are hurt by the emphasis placed upon it. Neither age group appears to have much information about the nondelinquents. The conclusion cannot be avoided that all the facts about all the teen-agers have not been made known.

When a problem exists and not all the facts related to it are known, we cannot be sure that the problem itself is accurately defined nor that our perspective about it is true. Most of the boys and girls sense that adult perspective about their age group is out of gear but they have no way of proving it. Adults do not seem to suspect that it might be. So let's look now at the statistical facts about all teen-agers to see if their hunch is right and also to test our own perspective.

What Are the Statistical Facts?

The U. S. census figures show that in 1950 there were over six million youth who were 15 to 17 years old and over eighteen million who were 18 to 25.

The teen-agers we are talking about are those in the 14 to 18 year age group which covers the normal junior and senior high school years. Because the census does not make this exact division we can only estimate how many boys and girls there are in this age grouping. A conservative estimate is seven million. This allows for the 14-year-olds who are not included in the first set of census figures and for the 18-year-olds who are still in high school. The facts we shall look at are mostly in percentages so that the relationship of the numerical facts will be accurate even if the figures are not precise.

Delinquency is a fact which must be faced, so we shall deal with its figures first. "The truth is that all of our delinquents add to less than 5 per cent of our juvenile population."[1] Some experts place it at 3 per cent. Recent reports predict that when the 1955 figures are in, the percentage will be higher. Even though the 5 per cent represents not only the teen-agers but some younger ones as well, let's be very conservative and double the higher percentage and make it 10 per cent, or 700,000 teen-age delinquents in the United States. A cause and cure for this kind of behavior must be found for the sake of the young person and for society.

Deducting this overgenerous allowance for the delinquents from the estimated 7,000,000 leaves *6,300,000* teen-age boys and girls who are not rated as a menace to themselves, to other teen-agers, or to adult society.

What about them? What are they doing? Let's look at some figures about them.

"In 1953, 2,000,000 of the 12-17 age group had some job, 3,000,000 in summer."[2] The vast majority of these also go to school and many of them are active in adult sponsored leisure-time youth programs as well.

"During the last twenty years, most leisure-time studies have estimated that 25% of the teen-age school youth belong to established youth organizations."[3] This means that almost two million of the nondelinquent boys and girls participate in organizational programs designed to help them establish themselves as reliable members of society.

The balance of slightly more than 4,000,000 either do not have the opportunity to join some group or do not choose to take advantage of whatever opportunities may be offered; and

---

1 "We're Raising a Great Crop of Kids." Jhan and June Robbins, *This Week Magazine*, N. Y. Herald Tribune, p. 7, Feb. 27, 1955.
2 "What's the Truth About Youth?" Bernice Bridges, *Adult Leadership*, June, 1955, p. 15.
3 *Ibid.*, pp. 15-16.

yet these boys and girls do not cause adults concern beyond the normal degree of adult bewilderment in dealing with the teen-age vicissitudes natural to the growing-up process.

Figures do not build adult confidence. But they do prove that the teen-age delinquents are in the minority and that the overwhelming majority of the boys and girls are not delinquent.

So let's take a bird's-eye view of what many boys and girls who seek and find value and citizenship training in established youth organizations are doing, in order to gain a quick impression of why adults who are associated with them have confidence in both the tapped and the untapped abilities and potentialities within this age group.

Most organizations have great difficulty in finding enough volunteer adults to help with the youth program. It seems safe to assume that the average adult is not aware of the leadership skills and experience of the democratic process that have been developed by young people. Boys and girls become increasingly aware of their citizenship responsibility. They become sensitive to racial and religious prejudice and attempt to do something about it in their own groups. They grow in world-mindedness because they are encouraged to learn about the United Nations. Most of them know more about its work than many adults do. Adult leaders frequently bring youth groups from other states to New York for several days of observation of the UN in action.

Thousands of adolescents are engaged in volunteer work in hospitals and social agencies. In some sections of the country such service is co-operatively sponsored by the schools which give recognition at graduation time or school credit in classes of social studies.

In many communities adults and youth are working co-operatively toward solutions to such troublesome problems as teen-age drinking, traffic accidents, and vandalism. They are also co-operating to obtain better schools, libraries, recreation centers, and playgrounds for younger children, and to set up summer work-experience programs.

A number of midwest states include teen-agers on official

adult state committees dealing with youth problems. Boys and girls help, too, to plan and participate with adults in an annual state conference on youth affairs. At least two states have an active, representative youth committee, interested in fostering adult-youth co-operation locally and state wide. The youth committee has an active working relationship with the adult Youth Committee. Detroit, for example, has teen-agers on the Mayor's committee on youth problems. Other large and small cities often call high school students in for consultation when the adults feel that the youth point of view about a pending decision should be heard.

Three national organizations having extensive youth programs include teen-agers on their national boards and on national committees related directly to youth programs. These are the National Council of YMCA's, the National Jewish Welfare Board, and the National Junior Red Cross. Many local units of these and other organizations follow the same policy.

All adults in contact with such teen-age energy and resourcefulness are convinced that widespread adult confidence in our teen-age group, as a whole, is long overdue.

Summary and Conclusions

The reality of present-day tensions, and the difficulty of meeting them with poise and spiritual fortitude have been recognized. We have established the fact that there is a relationship between the general atmosphere of tension and the "teen-age situation."

The seriousness of the delinquency problem has been acknowledged, and the necessity of finding a solution to it. At the same time, we have shown that the emphasis upon it, over a long time, has tended to reduce the normal degree of adult confidence in all teen-agers. It has also tended to reduce teen-age confidence in themselves and to generate, for them, a skepticism about adult willingness and ability to see the youth group in accurate focus. We gave evidence that mutual confidence between adults and young people too often is difficult and sometimes seems impossible to attain, but that without it adults cannot reach boys and girls to help them.

Our first conclusion is that there is no one teen-age situation but that there are, everywhere, *adult-youth* situations in which the problem of establishing mutual confidence exists. This conclusion leads to a new definition of the adult problem in relation to teen-agers: *How to achieve mutual confidence between adults and younger people in order that youth may freely accept the friendship of adults and that adults may adequately fulfill their responsibility to youth.*

We indicated, briefly, that this is possible to do. At the same time we gave evidence that there is an obvious lack of information about the good citizenship intentions and activities of the large majority of boys and girls who are not delinquent. This lack represents a previously unrecognized factor in the generalized "teen-age situation." It prevents a correction of any existing adult feeling that all teen-agers are out of hand. Such a lack of information tends to deny to the responsible ones the opportunity to prove their worth as an age group. Many young people sense that they should be able to do so, but with no available facts at their finger tips they feel unable to present a convincing case for themselves.

Our second conclusion is that a wide circulation of factual information about the present abilities and potentialities within the healthy teen-age group is a first and necessary step toward establishing a reasonable basis for that necessary adult confidence which can lead to mutual confidence between adults and teen-agers.

Since mutual confidence between persons and a co-operative partnership feeling is the goal in the development of human relationships in our form of society, we are convinced that information concerning the merits of youth will help both adults and teen-agers to reach for that goal. Therefore everything that follows is for the purpose of giving much needed information of two kinds: (1) that which will help adults to gain the necessary confidence in the abilities and potentialities of youth and (2) that which will show the improvement of relationship between the age groups whenever mutual confidence is achieved.

The second kind of information takes the form of telling true stories not only of mutual confidence but of a new and exciting feeling of partnership in working together in organizations and in communities to which they both belong.

None of the experiences can be exactly duplicated, but from them come some guideposts for establishing mutual confidence and a partnership feeling between the two age groups in any situation in which adults and teen-agers may find themselves.

CHAPTER 2

TEEN-AGERS AT WORK IN THEIR COMMUNITIES

This chapter provides many illustrations of adolescents who have tackled problems in the community and, with the assurance of adult confidence in them, have accomplished much. Section One tells four stories which reveal the opportunities provided by adults for boys and girls to show what they could do about (1) the teen-age traffic problem in Los Angeles, California; (2) a neighborhood vandalism situation in Cleveland, Ohio; (3) a community-wide vandalism difficulty in Alexandria, Minnesota; and (4) a New York City neighborhood narcotics situation.

In Section Two there is a full account of a project in Iowa City, Iowa, in which adults offered help to all teen-agers desiring summer employment. Ways are described in which youth and adults together developed and permanently established an annual summer teen-age work experience program.

Section Three tells stories in which adults offered all high school youth the opportunity for volunteer service with community social agencies in Louisville, Kentucky; in Cleveland, Ohio; and in Baltimore, Maryland.

SECTION ONE

Here are four stories which represent situations having three facts in common: (1) a community problem existed involving teen-agers, to which adults, by themselves, had been trying unsuccessfully to find a solution; (2) both adults and teen-agers had an interest and a stake in finding a satisfactory answer to the problem; (3) the problem was recognized separately by each age group, but when it was most acute neither the teen-agers nor the adults were aware of their mutual interest and concern about it nor were they aware of the possibility of working together to solve it. In each story some adult confidence in some teen-agers existed or developed; and from it mutual confidence grew through co-operative thought and action, because of which progress was made toward a solution of the problem.

A Teen-Age Traffic Problem in Los Angeles

The facts of this first story were sent by Miss Irene Shearer, Administrative Assistant to Mr. Ralph Fisher, Executive Secretary of the Los Angeles County Youth Committee, 1953-54. Miss Shearer is the professionally trained youth adviser to the Teen-Age Subcommittee about which the story centers.

The County of Los Angeles has had an all-adult Youth Committee for a long time. It is composed of seven professionally trained persons, each of whom is the administrator of an organization having an extensive youth program. The purpose of the committee is to discover youth needs and to find constructive ways to meet them. About six years ago the decision was reached to set up a teen-age subcommittee because the adults felt they might be able to do a better job if they had access to youth's point of view about the problems with which the committee had to deal.

(The organization of the youth subcommittee represents some adult confidence in the potential ability of teen-agers to contribute to the solution of social problems involving them.)

For several years the youth subcommittee functioned less well than the adults had hoped it would, for two reasons. First, a new subcommittee had to be organized each year because all the members were high school seniors, two from each organization represented on the adult committee. This meant that none of the fourteen new members knew each other nor were they familiar with what the preceding committee had done. Second, there was plenty of opportunity to talk, but little or no opportunity for action. Teen-agers love to discuss but become bored if they cannot "do something."

Two changes were made. The structure of the committee was changed so that seven seniors served for one year and seven underclassmen served for two years. This change assured a nucleus of boys and girls who knew each other and who were also familiar with the committee work.

(This move represents adult guidance in helping the committee to function better. The guidance was accepted because mutual confidence had developed between the adults and the teen-agers related to the two committees.)

The second change, initiated by the boys and girls themselves, represents growth in their confidence in themselves which was made possible because of the adult-youth confidence already achieved. They decided that rather than try to cover a wide range of interesting discussion subjects, they would pick one topic which was the number one interest of the group and would work on it for the full year. This decision, plus the choice of the topic "Teen-Age Traffic Problems," set the ball rolling toward a co-operative and productive experience with adults. It was an unexpected result directly related to the mutual, although different, stakes which both adults and teen-agers had in finding a solution to the problem. In California a driver's license can be obtained at sixteen. Safety and caution are not always a first consideration of all boys and girls of this age, and so traffic violations and accidents were running high. This fact represents the stake which the adults had in finding a solution. The boys and girls on the subcommittee were responsible young people, but they and others like them were being "lumped" with the irresponsible ones. They did not like this. The preservation of enlightened self-interest constituted the stake which the teen-agers had in finding a solution.

(Mutual adult-youth interest existed in the problem, but neither age group was aware of the fact when the teen-agers chose the topic.)

The subcommittee's first move was a decision to find the facts about the teen-age traffic situation in order to see what they could do about it. With the help of an officer of the State

Highway Patrol, who handled juvenile traffic offenses, the committee drew up a questionnaire on teen-age traffic problems and processed almost 2,000. The Los Angeles Board of Education tabulated the 1,200 questionnaires which were answered and returned to the committee.

(This step represents an extension of adult confidence in the subcommittee beyond that shown by the adult Youth Committee. It also represents the beginning of adult co-operation.)

The answers formed the basis for a Youth Forum on teen-age traffic problems, sponsored by a local newspaper, *The Los Angeles Times*. The forum was such an outstanding success that it brought an invitation to teen-agers to attend a Traffic Conference held by the Los Angeles Board of Education in the spring of 1953.

(These events demonstrate adult confidence extended to teen-agers other than those in the original small group.)

The conference included adults and 130 teen-agers representing sixty-five high schools in Los Angeles County. The adults and young people first met together in a general assembly. Four adults outlined the aspects of the problem which were to be discussed. The boys and girls met by themselves, in small groups during the morning, and the adults in the same way. Each youth group had an adult discussion leader and an adult resource person, qualified to answer questions about pertinent facts. During the afternoon the two age groups re-assembled. Ideas growing out of the small discussion groups were presented, and the young people had equal opportunity with the adults to present their ideas and conclusions. The adults were surprised and pleased because the teen-age ideas were so constructive and their enthusiasm in tackling the problem was so great.

(This adult reaction represents increased confidence in teen-age abilities. Teen-age confidence in adults was increased at the same time because they found out, during the conference, that adults were willing to listen to their ideas and, in doing so, found value in them. The trend, already started, toward mutual adult-youth confidence was strengthened.)

The reality of the increased adult confidence in teen-agers is substantiated by the fact that teen-agers were again invited to participate in a second traffic conference when the Governor's Traffic Commission met in Sacramento in the fall of 1953. Eighty boys and girls, representing high schools throughout the state accepted the invitation to share ideas with adults. Although the number of participating teen-agers was smaller than in the first conference, the representation covered a much wider geographical area. This was also true of adult representation. The results of this second conference were similar to those of the first one, but they represent a further extension of mutual confidence between the two age groups beyond the Los Angeles area where it first developed.

Within the Los Angeles area itself, increased adult confidence showed in another way. In October, 1954, the youth subcommittee was increased from fourteen to twenty members. Shortly after this a new adult advisory committee was organized. The purpose of this committee continues to be (1) to work with the teen-age committee and (2) to find further ways in which young people may have the opportunity to work co-operatively with adults. Another way was found quickly.

(The formation of this adult committee for the purposes stated shows that the experiences during the traffic conferences and the work which the teen-agers did leading up to them, provided an incentive for a nucleus of adults and teen-agers to cement the satisfactions gained from their new relationships and to extend the opportunities for more teen-agers and more adults to find a similar partnership feeling.)

The monthly Bulletin of the Los Angeles County Youth Committee dated February-March, 1954, reports that six members of the youth subcommittee participated with adults at the Youth Service Forum of the Welfare Planning Council. The purpose of the forum was to discuss teen-age needs and to determine the best ways to meet them. The report states that the young people made a number of concrete suggestions which were of value to the adult council. Among these was the suggestion that teen-agers are interested in finding work, especially in summer, but do not always know how to go about finding it. They indicated that they thought adults could help, and asked if they would be willing to do so.

When any teen-ager or a group of them *asks* for adult help in solving any problem of interest and importance to them— it is a sure sign that mutual confidence has been achieved.

No sudden and dramatic solution to the teen-age traffic problem resulted, but substantial progress was made in the direction of a solution. The real significance of this story is that many teen-agers and many adults found out step by step that they could trust each other; and they now know that by working together on any problem of mutual interest and concern, they can make more progress toward a satisfactory solution than either age group, working alone, could make.

A Neighborhood Vandalism Situation in Cleveland, Ohio

This second story took place in a neighborhood that included Patrick Henry High School in Cleveland, Ohio. The wrath of neighborhood adults was fully aroused, but they could not solve the problem alone. The teen-age action took place through the Student Council of the high school. The youth incentive for action was once again the fact that "all" teen-agers were judged responsible for the problem.

The story was sent by Dr. Alan Y. King, Supervisor of Social Studies, Board of Education. Written under the title "Let's Quit Being Vandals," by Bob Sterns, it was published in a small high school student paper called Good Citizens at Work. The original story has been shortened but otherwise unchanged in thought or language.

"LET'S QUIT BEING VANDALS"

It all started with snowballs crashing through house windows at the first big snowstorm of the year. Glass from smashed bus windows showered into the faces of two women riders. This was the last straw in a wave of teen-age vandalism, said the newspapers. Adults talked angrily about teen-age rowdy-ism. Editorials said, "These are the latest incidents of the wave of teen-age vandalism here. This behavior must be stopped, by the police, if necessary." The victims said, "They were students from Patrick High."

A meeting of the Student Council brought forth such remarks as "We're getting an awful reputation," and "You should see what I see in the soda shop where I work part time. Teen-agers from our school destroy and steal property, act like rowdies, and sass the manager. He asked me if the Student Council couldn't do something about it." The Student Council did.

They went about the problem in a businesslike way. They appointed a committee of eighteen students with a faculty adviser to try to separate fact from rumor. They first made a survey of neighborhood business men. This confirmed what the boy who worked in the soda place had said, and worse. Bus companies said that it cost them money constantly to repair broken windows and cuts made in upholstery, and to clean gum and lipstick off the upholstery. They said a lot of students try to get on the bus without paying their fare.

Movie people said it cost them $200 a week from damage caused by children in one way or another. "We have to lock our doors when school is dismissed so that students won't wreck our property." Of 20 business men questioned, 13 said that they had trouble controlling students who patronized their businesses.

The council found that others beside their students were involved and that it really was a neighborhood problem. So they called a meeting of student representatives from nine other schools, local merchants, city and police officials, community leaders, and even reporters.

The Student Council reported the result of the survey. Everyone had a chance to have his say. Opinions about what to do varied from putting it in the hands of the police to the idea that parents, teachers, and city officials should provide more recreational facilities.

But Franklin Trigg, President of the Student Council, said, "Our council thinks it's up to us teen-agers to solve this problem ourselves. Give us a chance, first. Let us do it our way here at Patrick High."

The Council's first move was to call a special school meeting to discuss the problem. Students and teachers together hammered out a plan for a campaign against vandalism. They decided to wake up the school to the idea that "good behavior means good citizenship." The students wrote and acted out a radio drama called "We the Pupils of Patrick Henry Want Order." It was broadcast over the school's public address system. Student-made signs appeared on the school's walls and bulletin boards. On the posters were snappy slogans like, "Be wise, behave, be popular," "It's not smart to be a show-off," "Have fun but use good manners."

The highlight of the campaign was a "Rate Yourself" Chart. The answers were frank. A third of the students admitted they had committed some act of vandalism. In analyzing the answers the Council found, however, that only a small percentage of the students were causing real trouble and that the largest number of offenders were in the eighth grade.

The Council decided that they should direct more of their thought and activities to the younger students. Adults helped. The police organized a Junior Police Club to provide sports programs for them. A neighborhood civic club conducted a survey to find out what kind of "after school" recreation facilities the students should have.

The story closes with the thought that there's room for much more improvement, but a check was made with the complaining merchants. They reported that teen-age behavior was much improved in many ways. A local newspaper said, "The Student Council has taken the first constructive step in combating the wave of crimes enacted by the youth in this neighborhood."

The "Rate Yourself" Chart which the Patrick Henry High School Student Council made and distributed among all the students, is given below.

HOW GOOD A CITIZEN AM I?

Circle your answer to each question and ask the above question of yourself.

1. When you are in public do you act as a good citizen should?

   Always   Usually   Sometimes

2. When with a group of friends, on the sidewalk, do you give space to others approaching you?

   Always   Usually   Sometimes

3. Are you considerate of others when you are in stores, delicatessens, movies, buses, or streetcars?

   Always   Usually   Sometimes

4. If you managed a business, would you welcome one who conducts himself as you do?

   Yes   No

5. Have you ever cut, scratched, marked, or destroyed public property?

   Yes   No

6. Do you annoy others by talking while seeing a movie?

   Usually   Sometimes   Never

7. Do you push or shove when boarding a public conveyance?

   Always   Usually   Never

8. Do you scuffle with friends on a bus or streetcar?

   Frequently   Rarely   Never

9. Do you try to get rides on buses or take merchandise from stores without paying?

   Usually   Sometimes   Never

10. Does your conduct in public contribute to the good name of your family, school, and community?

    Always   Usually   Sometimes

ANALYSIS OF THIS SECOND STORY

The change from lack of confidence in teen-agers to confidence in them follows the same pattern of development as in the previous story, but with several variations.

The first variation is that the change took place in a neighborhood. The second is that mutual confidence between adults and teen-agers first showed up within a public school rather than within a privately supported youth organization. The third is that the *teen-agers took the initiative* in taking the problem to the neighborhood adults.

Results were also achieved in a slightly different way:

1. Adults gave tacit consent to let the teen-agers do what they could—in their own way. (The newspapers gave full credit for teen-age initiative and accomplishments.)
2. The neighborhod adults saw new things to do which they had not seen until the teen-agers confronted them with all the facts in the problem situation.

Although each age group worked independently, doing whatever each could do that the other could not, a co-operative spirit and approach to the solution of the problem of concern to both age groups resulted from increased adult confidence in the responsible, neighborhood teen-agers.

A Community Vandalism Problem in Alexandria, Minnesota

This story is a condensation of the printed script of a tape recording made in Alexandria, Minnesota. The people are real; there were no actors used. The script was broadcast Sunday, June 8, 1952, over the CBS nation-wide network. The program was one of a series called "The People Act," presented by the TV-Radio Workshop established by the Ford Foundation and produced by CBS. Mr. Robert Trout was the narrator. Permission to use this condensation has been granted by Mr. Elmore McKee, Director of The People Act Center.

"THE PEOPLE ACT" IN ALEXANDRIA, MINNESOTA

Here is the situation as described by Mr. Robert Trout:

"This is the story of a letter that shook a small town to its roots. The town is Alexandria, Minnesota—population 6,500—120 miles northwest of St. Paul on the shores of Lake Agnes. They call Alexandria a ribbon town because its Main Street is State Highway 176. It is a summer resort town. Surrounded by lakes and farms. Two banks. Two theaters. Eight hotels. Thirteen churches. A 16,000-volume library. And six cops—including the chief—and Osterburg's.

"All the kids go to Osterburg's for a malted or a chocolate phosphate. It's an old-fashioned ice cream parlor with wooden booths and a big juke box up front. Mr. Osterburg is a round, sandy-haired man who wears rimless glasses and a brown pharmacist's coat. Clifford Hove is mayor.

"This is what the mayor thinks of the town:

'We think we've got a nice town here. That's City Hall up there to our left, and a post office is over on this side kitty corner across from City Hall. And down on this side we have Osterburg's. Richard Osterburg is a famous character around town and most other towns around the northwest.'

"Mr. Osterburg says, 'I've been here 30 years. In the restaurant business 50 years. It's the best city in the United States. Business is good. Nice lakes—210 lakes in our county. Fish in every lake. Why shouldn't we like this? Young people come in here, I think, more than any place in town.'

"Most of the adults in the town agree with Mr. Osterburg's estimate of Alexandria. But a spokesman for the younger generation takes a different view. A boy says:

'At night there is just nothing to do. You can't get started until about nine o'clock. You get out of a theater and there's no place to go except to your studies or home. About the only place you could go in the evening . . . we have a night . . . for instance the Elks News . . . we go down there and sit over a Coca-Cola or something and just sit and talk and talk and . . . go out in the street and just drum up something to do. And we get into trouble and probably go to Joe's down here to shoot a game of pool or something and we aren't of age. They throw us out of there and we go back out on the street and start breaking windows again.'

"In 1942 a ten o'clock curfew law was passed. To curtail the breaking of windows and to get the kids off the streets at night parents began talking about resurrecting and enforcing this old curfew law. This was the adult idea and it seemed good to them, but not to the boys and girls. The town began to hum and 'every boy and girl under 18 had an idea what they ought to do about the threat of the curfew.' Here is the tape recording of the conversation of some of the boys and girls:

"Hey, Lee, did you hear about the curfew they are putting on?" "Yeah, I guess I'll just have to go out tonight and do all I can because tomorrow there won't be much to do if you've got to get home so early."

"What're we going to do about play practice—it lasts until quarter to eleven just about every night." "Oh, the cops will get there and chase you out, I suppose. Dances have to be broken up and everything."

"Do you really think they can enforce this?" "Sure they can. They can enforce everything around here . . . the police." "You mean after play practice is over we'll have to go down to the clink for a while?" "It's about what will happen. It'll stay in force for a while but then the guys with cars will start going out of town and they'll be making their fun in other towns." "Well, what're we going to do about it? We can't just sit and twiddle our thumbs."

"Talk with our parents, but that doesn't do much good. They're pretty bullheaded."

"We could try a petition around . . . all the students sign and take it over to the police force and see what happens."

"I think that's a good idea. We've got to do something."

"I can see the papers tomorrow. . . . They'll probably have a stack of kids standing out in front of the police station and tell them they just herded in a bunch of delinquents that were caught out after ten o'clock."

"What do you think we can do now?"

"Well, I think our social class now are writing letters to government officials and I think if we could drop a line to Governor Youngdahl, it might help, I don't know."

"You write to him . . . You write to President Truman and see what you get."

Mr. Trout says the kids all laughed at Maynard Peterson's idea. Maynard even laughed at himself. But he sat down and wrote the letter anyway. Here is the letter:

My Dear Sir: The high school boys of Alexandria, like many boys throughout Minnesota, are disgusted with the problem of our city's recreation. There's a rumor that a 10-year-old curfew is soon going into effect by which the 18-year-olds and under must be in the hands of their parents by ten o'clock sharp. The way it is now, the public don't want them on the streets at night, and the business men of this area don't want them loitering in their places of business. If they aren't allowed in those places, I believe they will take to the alleys which is bad for any country as well as the city. If there is anything we could do to better our problems, we should like a reply from you. Sincerely yours, Maynard Peterson.

"Maynard's letter got into the local paper, and then the adults were shocked—and angry. Phones started ringing from the mayor's down to the ordinary citizen.

" 'After all, it seems to me that something like this should have been presented to a group of citizens or city fathers first.'

" 'Seems to me that the kids nowadays just think that they've got to have everything put down in black and white for them. They can't make their own fun like we did in years gone by.'

"They jumped on Maynard Peterson, too. He says, 'Immediately, the people around Alexandria here that I met on the street and through the high school kind of looked at me every time I turned around, and I think they were wondering just what kind of a guy I am. Some of them approached me in the restaurants and wherever I had business downtown, and they'd come in and ask me what the deal was. They criticized the letter; and, for instance, I was sitting in a café and one of the local business men approached me and criticized. Like he said, "Look, we have just built a nice ball park down here and a number of years ago, we built a tennis court down here and it's just . . . it's . . . well, the kids aren't backing it up." ' "

"Maynard Peterson hadn't expected that anything would happen but—. The climax came when Governor Youngdahl sent George Reed of the State Youth Conservation Commission up from St. Paul. That afternoon there was a meeting in the basement of the Library. Parents and youngsters jammed the room. There were no empty seats. County Attorney John McCarten acted as temporary chairman of the meeting. He explained that the meeting had been called as a result of Maynard Peterson's letter. The purpose was to give representatives from all organizations in the community as well as the young people a chance to express themselves on the question of whether or not there was an actual need for youth activities in the community or whether the community is taken care of in that respect. The adults and young people had divergent views, but most of the adults saw that something was wrong. Here are some tape recorded views expressed by boys and girls and adults:

MAN: I read the letter and I don't believe that the children do have a legitimate gripe, because after ten o'clock the children should be home with their parents, or with their parents.

GIRL: Well, I disagree with you there. I believe that the parents should certainly be with the children. But what are the children supposed to do when the parents themselves aren't home, and they have so many activities that take them away from home?

GIRL: Well, why can't we go bowling? Some of us kids had bowling in gym classes and we really liked it, but now we can't go into the bowling alleys at all.

GIRL: We need something exciting to do . . . something that we can do with everybody to have a lot of fun, not just sit around and worry about what we are going to do tonight. . . What's there to do? It's the same old things: go to the show, and go to Osterburg's, and then go home, and be sure you make it by ten o'clock, otherwise they'll probably send you home.

MAN: May I interrupt there, please? I don't see why the young people should be gallivanting around the street every night in the week anyway. It seems to me that there should be three or four nights a week that they could stay home. After supper sit down and read or take care of their music or hobbies such as whittling, art work, and things like that. I don't see why we should have such a problem about being out so much at night.

WOMAN: That's a point there. We planned a family picnic the other day . . . last Sunday . . . and we said, "All right, kids, let's all jump in the car," and we thought they'd be just delighted and they said, "Nothing doing—all the rest of our friends are going to the show; we don't want to go with the family on a picnic." So we got to . . . the youngsters seem to want to stick together in whatever they're doing. I think it's important to get their point of view. What would you really like? What would be ideal?

GIRL: Well, to provide activities that would include the youth of the whole community so that you're with all your friends and so that you can be . . . in different activities, not the same kind all the time like going to a show and then to Osterburg's. And that's about what it is, and there's nothing else to do. Plan something that's more varied, where everybody can take part.

GIRL: Well, if we have to be in by ten o'clock, why don't you give us a place to go where we can have some fun? We'd be willing to get in by ten o'clock if we had some fun before then. But when it lags all night. . . .

BOY: It takes all night to find a place to have fun. It just seems like ten o'clock comes around sooner than ever.

MAN: Well, could we say then that your problem is not only the curfew but lack of organized recreation in the entire community?

CHORUS: Yes!

"The adults realized that something needed to be done. The first thing they did was to form a Community Council and then a Youth Counncil. Three adults met with representatives of the school classes and got the Youth Council organized. The kids met and in their council they had more ideas about what could be done in Alexandria. These tape recordings speak for themselves:

BOY: Parents believe we should stay home, but we've got to let off steam somehow. I mean, we just can't sit home. Maybe in their old age they can sit home and talk over old times, but I know when they were young they let off a little steam too, and there's just nothing to let off steam on in this town.

GIRL: If they'd give us some place to have some recreation we'd show them that we could take care of it ourselves. But without nothing right now, how can we show them? Maybe they think we act like children; well, maybe we do, because there's nothing to do to show them we can act like adults. If they'd give us something sound and substantial to work on, we could show them.

"These ideas expressed in Youth Council, seemed to about sum up the youngsters' feelings. After a lot more discussion the group decided that a center of some sort was what it wanted and needed.

"There were many more meetings before the kids were ready to talk over their ideas with the adults. When the Youth Council met with the Community Council a woman made this comment, 'I'm sure it was the first time that the youngsters realized that adults were interested in their problem, and they didn't know quite how to react to us because they were so surprised that we were interested in them. And we tried to make them realize the force of the adults that were behind them.'

"The outcome of this joint meeting of adults and young people was that a committee of ten, adults and youth, was appointed to make a survey of the town's recreational facilities. They rang doorbells to find out individual adult attitudes. They found out that the high school had 52 per cent rural and 48 per cent town children. They found that one-fourth of the mothers of the town children worked outside the home. The rules governing bedtime hours and number of nights out varied from very strict to no rules at all. They also found that one-third of the children belonged to no group at all. The young people found that there were many adult organizations in town, some with space for youth activities but none had made the space available. None had any youth program except the women's club which offered prizes for essays on conservation.

"As a result of frequent reports on the findings of the survey committee, organizations gradually became aware of the need of more facilities for the young people and provided them.

"The ultimate result was the decision to build a youth center. The place was selected—the kids got the center going. They decorated, painted, made curtains and furniture. The adults hired a recreation director, appropriated $8,000 a year, set up a recreation department in the town to work out a long-range program for the kind of recreation the kids wanted."

Mr. Trout sums it all up: "It took three years. It took hard work and sometimes it went slowly. But nobody talked about a curfew any more—and nobody talked about breaking windows. Maynard Peterson, out of high school, a PFC in the Army now, came home on furlough, looked around and wrote another letter telling Judge Youngdahl what had happened in three years since his first boyish letter was sent to him as the then governor of Minnesota."

Mr. Trout closed the program in this way: "Elapsed time between letters: three years. Distance: from a broken window to a brand-new youth center and a full recreation program. In three years the people of Alexandria have come to grips with the problem they hadn't even known existed, and have started to solve it."

AN ANALYSIS OF THE ALEXANDRIA STORY

The process of achieving that adult-youth mutual confidence which can lead to co-operative thought and action is the same in this as in the two previous stories, but this one shows two variations in detail within the process that are different from those already indicated in the preceding illustrations.

In this adult-youth community problem situation, the young people had no youth organization through which to gain sufficient self-confidence to make them feel there was something they could do about it. All those who were not contributing to the vandalism felt the unfairness to them of the proposed adult solution. They saw quite clearly that the proposal was no solution at all because those who so desired could find ways of getting around the curfew and those who wanted to abide by the law even if they didn't like it, would pay an unreasonable price in doing so. The teen-age majority not only lacked confidence in themselves but lacked confidence in the willingness of community adults to listen to their point of view. All were utterly discouraged—all, that is, except one boy.

This one boy was mature. He had confidence in himself and courage to do what he could see to do. He also had confidence in *one adult* who happened to be the Governor of Minnesota.

Because this one important and busy adult was willing to listen to one boy who felt confidence in him (indicating his confidence in the boy) *the rest of the discouraged teen-agers gained the opportunity to be heard also.*

This story incidentally illustrates three points to be remembered: (1) that discouraged attitudes are contagious; (2) that everybody, including teen-agers, must sometimes pay a price for standing alone against the majority; and (3) that teen-age abilities are not limited to young people who have the opportunity for adult guided youth-group experience. The abilities of those who do not have that opportunity merely take longer to show up because there are fewer chances to gain practice in group thinking and action which would develop self-confidence.

A Narcotics Problem in a New York City Neighborhood[1]

The original settlers of the East Harlem neighborhood, in New York City, were men and women of Italian origin. In recent years there has been a large influx of people from Puerto Rico. Language difficulties and differences in social standards and customs make life more than ordinarily complicated.

The confusion and uncertainty among the people increased

[1] Condensation of a report read at the National Conference of Social Work, June 4, 1953, by Miss Mildred Zucker, Executive Secretary of the James Weldon Johnson Community Center in New York City.

to a high-tension degree during 1951 and 1952 because of the construction of new low-cost housing units. Old dwellings were being torn down to make way for the new. In the midst of the new development the James Weldon Johnson Community Center was in the process of construction.

"Before the center was opened, groups of teen-agers, some of whose houses had been torn down, were hanging around the doors wanting to know if they would be welcome." Miss Zucker and her staff said, "Yes," little knowing at the time that "these eager teen-agers waiting at the door were members of one of the most feared gangs in East Harlem. Their problems expressed themselves in gang fights with guns and knives, truancy, stealing, sex delinquency, and narcotics. The staff was trained in settlement work but had had no experience with gangs. . . .

"We realized that it was impossible, at least at first, to develop a program in which these seriously disturbed youngsters should mingle freely with the better-adjusted ones. We chose the gangs, but eventually we were able to serve the normal groups too, by instituting a separate and different program with meetings on nights when the gangs were not there."

Here is the story which resulted from "choosing the gangs." It is a story full of adult compassion and confidence even in the "bad" teen-agers and one which also shows superb judgment, common sense, lack of a defeatist attitude, and true wisdom on the part of the staff. No untrained adult should attempt to duplicate this kind of effort, but any adults should feel heartily ashamed of themselves if they do not do their share toward guiding and co-operatively helping the healthy nondelinquent teen-agers in their own communities. The story follows in the words of Miss Zucker's report.

HOW THE STAFF MADE HEADWAY WITH THE GANG TEEN-AGERS

Our approach to these youngsters was one of friendliness and acceptance. This showed itself in many ways—going to court when a youngster got in trouble, helping him to get a job, arranging for medical and psychiatric treatment, writing to a boy away from home, preventing a fight by negotiating with our group and an opposing gang, or, just sitting and listening to legitimate complaints about the attitudes of the police in the neighborhood, discrimination, and other unfair practices to which our teen-agers were subjected.

In the beginning they saw the center only as a place to keep warm. But then when the weather got warm and they still stayed on, they said, "It's nice here, you call us by our first names . . . you help us stay out of trouble and help us if we get in trouble . . . we can run dances, play games and have a good time here . . . and we trust you. We know you don't go to the cops." In other words, they recognized our complete acceptance of them. This fact made it gradually possible to do something about the narcotics problem.

This did not all happen overnight. It actually took two years of club activity, club council work, and individual service to achieve the degree of confidence which made it possible for the teen-agers to want to suggest the formation of a narcotics committee.

Once the committee was formed there were other factors, besides their trust in us, which helped the youngsters know how to work effectively. These factors were their own highly organized gang experiences, their participation in clubs and councils where they developed the ability and practice of speaking up when they had ideas, planning and carrying through satisfying and socially acceptable activity. Actually only a small number of the membership took part in the narcotics committee activities, but, there was almost complete approval of the committee by the entire membership. There was beside this, a kind of pride in the eventual prestige and recognition which "their" center received from the larger community.

WHY THE TEEN-AGE NARCOTICS COMMITTEE WAS FORMED

The top year for reported cases of the use of narcotics was 1950 according to the Public Health Records.

We became aware of the spread of the use of narcotics in the fall of 1950 when a student club leader reported talk by the youngsters of the use of the "stuff." Their language was guarded, and no names or places were ever mentioned. As the members gained confidence in the student leader, they talked more openly about it. Some of the girls were worried because their boy friends used it. They finally talked to members of the center staff about it.

Early in 1951, when dances were extended to midnight, we noted that after 10:30 P.M. heads began to droop and we became convinced that narcotics were the cause. There was general recognition of the problem but no community-wide action took place. Informal discussions between the staff and center members continued until April, 1951.

At that time the Teen-Age Council agreed that it might be a good idea for the staff to invite a psychiatrist to talk to the membership about the use of drugs. Their reaction to the talk was that he was "too easy" because he talked only about the causes and effects of drugs without placing blame or guilt on the users.

During May evidence was established that made it fairly certain that there were at least eight users among the active membership of the center. The girls, especially, were concernd about "doing something." It was obvious that if the situation were reported to the police, all hope of doing something would evaporate because the youngsters would feel that confidence had been broken, the trust which had been so long in the making would be destroyed. For the same reason parents could not be approached at this time either. During December, 1951, a series of meetings was held with the Teen-Age Council and Staff of the Center. In the course of these meetings a definite plan of action was evolved.

The plan agreed to with the youngsters was this: that a general membership meeting should be called and at the meeting the staff should (1) announce that letters to probable users would be written asking them to come in for personal interviews, and (2) explain to them that they could either accept psychiatric help, or be barred from the use of the center for all but gym activities. Two of the eight accepted help, two were already receiving help elsewhere, one was sent out of the country by his parents, one went to Puerto Rico, and two left the center. The important significance of this action by the staff—resulting from consultation with the Teen-Age Council about a plan of action—was a sense of relief among the membership and such comments as, "You sure picked the right ones," and then, "Why don't we form a teen-age committee to see what we can do to help, but the staff should pick the committee."

THE FORMATION OF THE COMMITTEE AND THE FIRST STEPS TAKEN

The original narcotics committee was made up of the president of the Teen-Age Council, two other boys, and three girls. They met weekly. After three meetings they asked and secured permission from the Teen-Age Council to hold a meeting for parents on the night of the regular Council dance. The Council agreed to give up the hall for the meeting. One hundred twenty-three letters were written and sent to all parents. Five parents, fifteen teen-agers, and three members of the adult council showed up, but two parents were added to the teen-age committee.

Two months later another meeting, a neighborhood one, was held. Fifty-five people came, including teen and adult representatives of the center, school and church people, representatives of the Juvenile Aid Bureau, Narcotics Squad, District Attorney's office, and probation officers.

The purpose of this meeting was to find out what was actually being done in the neighborhood. Officials praised the efforts of the teen-age committee, but offered no concrete suggestions beyond the importance of reporting sellers. It was discovered that nothing was being done in an organized way by others in the neighborhood. At the close of the meeting thirty-five center parents and teen-agers were asked to remain to discuss what could be done on a neighborhood basis. This discussion resulted in the formation of a Community Narcotics Committee made up of eighteen teen-agers and ten parents.

ACTION TAKEN BY YOUTH AND ADULTS TOGETHER

A concrete program, followed out to the letter, was initiated for the balance of 1951. This program included the following objectives:

1. To provide parent information, in particular, and community information, in general, about narcotics, in relation to where the kids buy it, how to detect its use, where to go for help, and simple and safe ways to report sellers.
2. To hold a mass meeting to arouse interest, to secure more members for the committee and to publicize the need for more action on the part of the Federal Narcotics Bureau.
3. To visit the new teen-age narcotics hospital in order to get first-hand information, for passing on to those who need it, about what treatment was available and what the treatment was like.

During the carrying out of this program 300,000 leaflets and 200 posters in English and Spanish were prepared. They were distributed by teens and adults, many of whom were not even on the committee. These informational pieces told, in printed form, what the committee thought people would want to know about narcotics and the problems connected with its use. The distribution of this great quantity of material took place in one day. All the stores, schools, other centers, and houses in the neighborhood were covered by the distributors.

The mass meeting was held in the school and was attended by more than four hundred people, adults and youth. Jackie Robinson came to the meeting as a guest speaker. The meeting was presided over by the teen-age chairman who gave a "most stirring address." Petitions for action were signed, and money contributed for committee activity. Five college girls and three members of a family who had been helped were added to the committee.

RESULTS BEGIN TO SHOW

We continued to get reactions to the leaflets for months after their distribution. Requests for copies came from students, members of the Narcotics Squad, the National Security Agency, the State Mental Health Commission, the State Youth Commission, and other social agencies in the city. Letters and telephone calls from parents came in, asking for help. Requests for the leaflet also came from other states and from Canada.

We began to notice from the newspapers that an intensive drive was going on against big "dope" sellers and from reports from the District Attorney's office that there was an increase in "valid complaints."

Lest our efforts be enlarged beyond our abilities and defeat our original purpose, we made it abundantly clear "that the interest of our committee was *to help teen-agers* and not to become an arm of the Narcotics Squad. Some of the youngsters, overwhelmed by the success of their efforts, began thinking that they could be a secret service division of the law. *The others convinced them that this was not our job.*"

The proposed visit to the Riverside Hospital for teen-age narcotics users was carried through at the end of March. Much that was good was discovered. It was also obvious that it was very inadequate in facilities for meeting the emotional and social needs of the patients while they were undergoing treatment. The failure of society to meet these needs in a healthy, active, and satisfying way is one of the underlying causes of drug addiction in teen-agers.

Miss Zucker says, "The teen-agers took the initiative and held it all the way . . . by the end of the year I felt that the committee had already done all it could do. But they were not ready to quit. Early in January, 1953, stories appeared in the newspapers about the possible closing of the teen-age narcotics hospital. The committee sat in session and outlined what was wrong with the hospital. They wrote a letter to the Mayor and subsequently were quoted in the New York *Herald Tribune* on their urgent request for the continuance of the hospital. . . .

We have now reached the point where the committee feels it has a permanent place and a long job to do in the community."[2]

AN ANALYSIS OF THE FOURTH STORY

As this story of East Harlem unfolded it was difficult to visualize what other less skilled adult leaders would have done if faced with a similar situation. It almost goes without saying that the average adult, untrained in youth work, should not try to deal with such a complicated problem as teen-age narcotic addiction, but they can give moral and financial support to those who are trained and who are trying to help not only young people already addicted but also those for whom the drug habit is a problem within their families or close acquaintances.

That the process of achieving mutual confidence is always the same regardless of the kind of youth with whom adults become associated and regardless of the type of situation, is demonstrated in this narcotics problem story. It should do much to increase adult confidence in any individual teen-agers or any group of them within the teen-age majority and even in the potentialities of those who are not, because it shows:

1. That nondelinquent boys and girls are capable of feeling responsibility to help those who are delinquent, and that with adult backing they can do so.
2. That teen-age abilities are not limited by virtue of race, color, nationality background, or social or economic status.
3. That those who may feel handicapped because of their differences stand to gain much and perhaps more from adult sponsored and guided youth programs than those who are not so handicapped.
4. That it is essential to accept each boy or girl *as he is,* whether or not we like what he does, and to believe in his potentialities for improved behavior and constructive activ-

[2] As of July, 1955, the hospital had not been closed. It seems impossible to believe that the teen-age interest and ability to help tackle the narcotics problem failed to exert influence upon the decision to keep the hospital open.

ity. To do this is the essence of the meaning of adult confidence in a teen-ager. The importance to the boy or girl of
acceptance increases in direct proportion to the seriousness
of the young person's problem for him, and to the seriousness of the behavior resulting from the problem.

5. That apart from mutual confidence, no adult guidance can
   or will be accepted by any individual teen-ager or by a
   group of them, and that adult confidence must come first.

And finally, this story should be a source of encouragement
to all adults because, if mutual confidence can develop in this
more difficult kind of situation than most of them will encoun-
ter, they may feel assured that it *can* develop in the more normal kinds of situations in which adults and teen-agers are most
likely to find themselves.

SECTION TWO

The first group of stories in this chapter revealed how some
initial adult confidence in teen-agers provided an opportunity
for action on their part; how mutual confidence gradually
developed and co-operative action resulted when a community
problem existed in whose solution both age groups had a stake.

The following story illustrates how this same process applies
when young people have a problem that is important to them
but not necessarily to the community or to the adults, beyond
the desire of some adults to help them, if they can, and a sense
of responsibility to try to do so.

Iowa City's Teen-Age Employment Service and Work Experience Program

Here is the story of how the Woman's Club in Iowa City,
Iowa, offered an opportunity to teen-agers to have summer
work experience and how co-operative adult-youth thinking
and action produced what has now become a permanent community program.

Other communities have developed similar programs, but this story was chosen because a complete, detailed report was available. We can only summarize here the highlights of the program. This condensation of the original report has been edited and approved by Mrs. Myrtle S. Hubbard, the first director of the program, and author of the full report. It has also been approved by the Youth Employment Organization Committee of the Iowa City Woman's Club. The condensation follows.

The program was approved and financed by the Iowa City Woman's Club as its major youth conservation project for 1951. The approximate cost to the club for that first year was $100. The program is now on a permanent basis and is self-supporting. The beginnings of the program were based on three approaches: (1) To rouse the public to its responsibility to provide work as well as play for the teen-agers; (2) To educate youth to the proper work attitudes and to teach him what an employer has a right to expect from him as an employee; (3) To educate the employer as to his responsibility in hiring teen-agers, so that they may be treated as just what they are— beginners in the economic field.

THE BACKGROUND REASONS FOR THE PROGRAM

"TEEN-AGERS VANDALIZE FRATERNITY HOUSE"— these were headlines in an Iowa City newspaper during the summer of 1950. The community shook its collective head. One of the police officers remarked, "What Iowa City needs is more recreation for its kids. They need to be kept busier; then they wouldn't get into so much mischief."

But the members of the Woman's Club thought that they had a better remedy. One mother of three said, "Recreation, phooey! What these kids need is not more recreation, but more occupation. One must create before he recreates. One must *work* before he is able to appreciate play."

They looked around Iowa City to see what was being done for its youngsters. It looked like a pretty good picture. There was a tax supported recreation center. There was a new swimming pool. Supervised playgrounds were in various parts of the city under paid directors. The Scout programs were going strong, supported by the Community Chest. So were the YMCA and YWCA programs. Each of the churches had a "Youth" program and most of the service clubs and lodges were doing something in the way of keeping youth busy.

Iowa City had assumed its responsibility to provide recreation for its youth's leisure time. But what about the time in between? Should teen-agers have all leisure time in the summer, with no feeling of responsibility in the community—no chance to use their muscles and their brains in the productive fields of activity of the town? Didn't Iowa City *owe* its teen-agers a chance to *work* as well as *play*?

The clubwomen reasoned, "Our American way of life is no accident. We have built our country and our freedom on men who have created their *own* freedom by using their hands as well as their heads. Men have found pride and satisfaction in doing their work well. *Work* is an American heritage. Iowa City boys and girls have a *right* to be given a chance to learn to earn."

The women were convinced that their idea was sound, but two questions had to be answered before any program could be worked out. They had to find out what opportunities for work experience were available to teen-agers and whether or not the boys and girls wanted to work.

When the teen-agers were consulted, the answer was almost unanimous, "Give us a chance." They said that most high school students wanted jobs but "we don't know how to find them."

Iowa City is not an industrial town. It has a population of about thirty thousand including the 10,000 students of the State University of Iowa. The State Hospitals are there too, but no large industries. A number of adults had tried hiring teen-agers other summers. They were not enthusiastic about trying again. The women found, however, that in each case the boys or girls had not been adequately informed as to exactly what was expected of them.

Although the prospects of finding jobs for teen-agers were not very bright, the adults refused to be discouraged. They also insisted upon taking the teen-agers at their word when they said they did want to work. So the women went to work vigorously and systematically.

THE FIRST STEP

A general community meeting was called by the Woman's Club. Those in attendance in addition to the club members included high school faculty members, employers, university faculty members interested in youth problems, the local office manager of the Iowa State Employment Service, and—last but not least—representative teen-agers.

The meeting was a discussion type with all, including the teen-agers, having their say. Two conclusions were reached: (1) a summer work program was desirable and possible if all worked together to produce it; (2) a community committee consisting of adults and teen-agers should be appointed to work out the details for such a program.

THE WORK OF THE COMMITTEE

The first thing which this committee did was to make a survey of all students in the four Iowa City high schools totaling 976 boys and girls, to determine specifically the number who desired work and any preferences with regard to the type of work they wanted. The teen-agers took responsibility for distributing and collecting the questionnaires and helped with the tabulation of the answers. The results of the survey showed that 210 boys and 176 girls had part-time jobs during the school year and 54 boys and 78 girls had already lined up jobs for the summer. Three hundred and fourteen girls and one hundred and sixty-five boys said that they would appreciate community help in getting jobs for the summer. This added up to a total of 497 boys and girls who really wanted to work during the summer.

This meant that many employers had to be found. It seemed important to the committee that the purposes of the program should be clearly stated before any prospective employers were approached. This is the way the purposes were stated:

1. To provide a medium for teen-agers to secure employment for the summer vacation months so that they might learn to be successful workers and desirable members of society.
2. To secure employers through whom these young people entering the field of labor would find guidance, security, and understanding.
3. To encourage proper attitudes toward work and to teach satisfaction in achievement.
4. To help young people develop good work habits.
5. To assist in establishing work records to be filed, that they might be available to youth for future reference.
6. To establish a youth-adult partnership in community action, to the benefit of both, as a means of maintaining and strengthening our freedom and democratic way of life.
7. To impress upon youth that it "belongs" and has an important responsibility in the community.

Armed with this tangible, interpretative statement of purpose for the program which could eliminate any possible misunderstanding about it, the co-operation of all community organizations, newspapers, radio, the University of Iowa, the churches, labor unions and theaters was sought and obtained.

Of specific importance was the support of the labor unions and their offer of help. One hazard in developing a teen-age work program is the possibility of violation of child labor laws. The unions helped very much in eliminating this hazard. All existing labor laws were fully investigated by the county and city attorneys, and reports filed.

In developing a program of this kind adults have some responsibilities for teen-agers which youth cannot assume for themselves. One of these is responsibility for safeguarding the welfare and morals of the boys and girls who are employed. A thorough investigation was made of all types of businesses which might employ teen-agers to make sure that they were desirable from this point of view. A club member who was a former truant officer conducted the investigation. A list of 250 prospective employers who could be depended upon was compiled.

Subsequently a mimeographed letter was sent to each prospective employer enclosing an "enlistment" card. These were addressed to be returned to the State Employment Service by mail.

The "enlistment" form which the committee worked out follows:

(Please return, even if co-operation is impossible)

I want to co-operate in Iowa City's Youth Work Experience Program ....

I will provide work for .... boys .... girls.

Nature of job ....

Hours ....

Where ....

Pay offered ....

Where youth may apply ....

Ask for ....

Are you employing any teen-age help?............................

How many? ....

Remarks and suggestions;

Signed...

THE TEEN-AGERS SUGGEST AN IDEA

Even though the boys and girls could not possibly see all the hours of work which the adults put in, they were grateful for what they could see. They were eager not to let the adults down and they wanted to do a good job when they became employed.

Because this teen-age attitude was general, they proposed that a "basic training" program be instituted in order that they could be as well prepared as possible before their jobs started. The idea suggested itself because of the U. S. Army policy of basic training which precedes all specific assignments to military duty. The training program was developed on the basis of what the teen-agers themselves felt they needed to know.

THE ESSENCE OF THE BASIC TRAINING PROGRAM

Pre-employment discussions were held at the office of the Iowa State Employment Service; effort was made to help the teen-agers feel that there was dignity in menial work; business men gave their points of view about what they felt they had a right to expect from employees and their responsibilities to those whom they employed. A number of films were found helpful. Among these were:

How to Keep a Job
Finding the Right Job   Coronet Instructional Films
Choosing Your Occupations   65 East Water Street
Aptitudes and Occupations   Chicago 1, Illinois

Finding Your Life Work   Carl F. Mahnke
                                215 East Third Street
                                Des Moines 9, Iowa

The final result of this teen-age idea of a basic training course was the production of a booklet entitled "How to Win Jobs and Influence Bosses."

THE FINAL STEP BEFORE LAUNCHING THE PROGRAM

It was necessary to work out some practical method of job placement for the 497 teen-agers who wanted to work. This is the plan finally adopted.

A central placement office seemed essential. The Iowa State Employment Service volunteered the use of its personnel and office, which was already set up for such purposes. Its local office manager, herself a mother and interested in youth and their attitudes toward work, gave invaluable advice, service, and counseling.

All questionnaires from the original survey were filed in that office, thus eliminating the need for further application except in the case of some teen-ager who had not answered one.

In such cases the job application was made on the regular form used by the employment service.

When job openings came in, the office tried to fit the youth to the job. Personal telephone calls were made to the youth, telling of the opening. If the young person was not available or was uninterested, a general announcement was made over the public address system in each high school. The applicant then went directly to the State Employment Office for further information and placement, if desired.

In each case the manager gave personal counseling to the youth as to conduct expected on the job and his responsibility to himself, to his employer, and to the community in accepting it.

THE PROGRAM IS LAUNCHED

In June, 1951, just before the schools closed, a final survey was made. This showed that 727 teen-agers had jobs for the summer. The women could have easily become discouraged in the beginning, but they did not. Their faith in the idea and confidence in the teen-agers' sincerity when they said they wanted work not only kept the women doggedly going but drew many more adults into the co-operative process which included the wholehearted effort of the teen-agers themselves.

A MIDSUMMER CHECK-UP

About mid-July, after the young people had a chance to become adjusted to their jobs, a team of women, chosen for their understanding and tact, called on each employer to ask for a report of the youth's performance "on the job." If the report was satisfactory, it was filed with the State Employment Service, the young person was told of the satisfactory report, and the parents were told of their child's success. If the report was unsatisfactory, an experienced counselor discussed his difficulties with him. He was then given another chance when an opening occurred. It is significant that there were only a few such instances.

A FINAL EVALUATION

In September, after school started, a final survey was made. A few items in the final summary are of special interest to us:

1. Police reported a minimum of trouble with teen-agers.
2. Approximately 887 of the original 984 surveyed had been employed.
3. The community expressed appreciation of this new adult-youth partnership and desired continuation of the program indefinitely.
4. The City Council and six city commissions invited teen-agers to become ex-officio members of these bodies.
5. The Board of Education invited two teen-agers to sit on the board as ex-officio members.

These last three items are of particular interest because they further confirm the results observable in our first group of stories, namely:

When adults have enough confidence in teen-agers to offer them the opportunity to do something about a problem of concern to them, and adults help co-operatively, the teen-agers justify the adult confidence in them. Both adults and teen-agers experience satisfaction in their new relationship, and more adults in the community gain confidence in boys and girls. This confidence is expressed in concrete ways, such as giving teen-agers opportunities to carry additional kinds of community responsibility.

This story also illustrates an adult understanding of a basic teen-age need to achieve independence. The adolescent concept of independence includes the right to make decisions on matters of real concern to them and the right to make mistakes and learn to profit by them. The clubwomen recognized the teen-age right to accept or reject their offer of help in finding summer work. It was the way in which the offer was made that influenced the boys and girls to accept it rather than turn it down.

The clubwomen were convinced that work experience "would be wonderful for the kids,"[3] and with that conviction and their reasons for it they might have approached them somewhat like this: They could have made speeches to them in high school assembly saying in attitude, "The trouble with you kids is that you need to work for a change instead of wasting your time playing all summer." With this approach, teen-age feelings about their right of decision in the matter would have been outraged. They would have bristled separately and collectively. Almost any one of them would have said at least to himself: "Work, phooey! Why should I work? My parents are supposed to support me, and anyhow I work all winter going to school. Why shouldn't I have some fun?" This reaction is typical when the adult approach is demanding and smacks of criticism.

But these clubwomen were wise in the ways of teen-agers. Their attitude said, "Look, we have a hunch that a lot of you kids would like to work this summer. What about it? Because —if you would—we think we can help you to find work and we would like to if we may." The teen-age reaction to this approach was also typical. If they had not been interested they would have sensed the genuine adult interest and would have been honest enough to say they were not. Instead, their almost unanimous responsive attitude said, "Gee, we sure do want to work. Do you mean it? Will you help us?" and then, "What can we do about it ourselves?"

Parents who have experimented with this type of approach whenever circumstances allowed know that this adolescent reaction is the usual one. Adults experienced in youth work also know that these teen-age attitudes rarely fail to show up whenever the adult adviser offers help in a co-operative spirit rather than in a dictatorial one. This does not mean that teen-agers do exactly what adults want, but it does mean that the adult suggestion or offer of help is accepted for what it is worth. Thus the chance is created for adults to add construc-

[3] "Teen-Age Employment and Work Experience Program," Youth Employment Organization Committee, Iowa City, Iowa, p. 5.

tive ideas to those which teen-agers may have, and between them a better plan usually evolves than either adults or teen-agers had thought of.

We firmly believe that there are times when the responsibility of decision must rest on the adult. All we are implying here is that because of the universal adolescent need for independence and for growth, all decision-making situations involving teen-agers should be weighed to decide whether real harm could come from their wrong decision or only a painful mistake from which they could learn. If real harm would result, then adults must assert their authority and stick to it with a complete and frank explanation of it; but if only the chance to learn from a mistake is obvious, it is the better part of wisdom to let them go ahead with their choice. As this story shows, the attitude of approach used by the women influenced the boys and girls toward rather than away from something that "would be good for them."

That the clubwomen did consciously recognize the teen-age need for independence is substantiated by the following excerpt from a letter received from Mrs. Hubbard on August 21, 1955:

It seems significant to me that this program has been continued with variations for the past five years. . . . The Optimist Club has joined forces with the Woman's Club, hiring a teen-age girl in the placement office for those under sixteen. . . . We have found that our program has done exactly what we wanted. Our community is now educated to recognize the need of our teen-agers for summer jobs. *The boys and girls go out "on their own" and get their own jobs.* Our job is now mainly one of publicity even though we still maintain a placement service for those under sixteen.

SECTION THREE

This section illustrates teen-age interest in and ability for assuming real responsibility in a community's social service agencies. The following stories show what young people did and are doing with the opportunity which adults had enough confidence in them to offer.[4]

Louisville, Kentucky's High School Social Service Program

The material for this first story was sent by Mrs. Ralph P. Long, Secretary of the Volunteers Bureau of Louisville, Kentucky, through 1954. In addition to the material about how the program works, she sent a large sheaf of letters from boys and girls who had written to the bureau expressing appreciation for the opportunity which had been offered them. Excerpts from a few of the letters are quoted.

The project is called "The High School Social Service Program." It has been in operation for close to twenty-five years. It is sponsored by the Volunteers Bureau, a department of the Health and Welfare Council of Louisville. It is not a part of the school curriculum, but it is approved by the Board of Education and encouraged by the teachers in the school.

HOW THE PROGRAM WORKS

As a first step, representatives from all the social agencies describe their separate programs to all the students in the high school during a general session. A series of training sessions are held in the school during the school season and at the agency during the summer.

These sessions follow a definite pattern. First, the course is given a theme. For example, the 1952 fall sessions were called "Good Citizens at Work" and the 1953 spring session was called "Training for Good Citizenship." The first session is always one of orientation which gives background information about what social service is and why it can be better understood by participating in it.

Each of the following sessions is devoted to just one agency

[4] Reports of similar programs were received from South Philadelphia, Pa.; the Walton High School, New York City; Memphis, Tenn.; and San Francisco, Calif.

in the community. The director of the agency "gives the course," assisted by other staff members when there are departments within the service suitable for teen-age volunteer service. For example, the children's hospital has a separate department of physical therapy in which teen-agers can be trained to help. The adults are frank. They pull no punches with regard to the quality of work expected or the kind of responsibility to be placed upon the young person who undertakes it.

At the close of the entire series each student who has attended at least five of the sessions and is still interested, fills out a formal application blank indicating the first and second choice of agency for volunteer work. Effort is made to give each one his or her first choice. The students sign up for a minimum of 28 hours and receive a certificate of credit upon graduation from high school. Because there has been co-education in the high school for only a short time the volunteers have been mostly girls up to now.

Each agency is responsible for giving the specific training needed after the young person starts the volunteer job. "The training is given on a regularly scheduled basis and is a little more intensive than the training given to adults. Assignments in the agency of the young person's choice are comparable to adult assignments; in fact, the agencies prefer the students in many instances."

The annual report of the Volunteers Bureau for 1952 indicates that 127 teen-agers fulfilled volunteer requirements and assignments in 17 community chest agencies, and that 220 did the same in 23 noncommunity chest agencies, to make a total of 347 teen-agers and 1,582 adults.

A news clipping from the *Louisville Courier-Journal* dated June, 1953, states that the students and faculty of the J. M. Atherton High School received the Freedom Foundation award for outstanding social service. The Foundation annually recognizes outstanding school projects which use the community as a laboratory for citizenship training. This award was given for the 1952-53 school year when 96 of Atherton's 163 students received certificates for volunteer social service work.

In September, 1954, a new opportunity was offered to the teen-agers. "Fifty of them enrolled in the Ground Observer Corps at the Air Filter Center. Of this number, forty registered for a six months' advanced course. The Air Force officers who conduct these courses say that they like to work with the student group and feel that they have greater stability than the adult volunteers."[5]

That the young people themselves appreciate the experience of social service responsibility can be felt through the following excerpts from teen-age letters sent unsolicited to the Volunteers Bureau:

1. *From a volunteer in a hospital for crippled children:* "Their parents are only allowed a short visit once a week, so the children are all eager and friendly when I come in. I love this work and wouldn't trade my experiences for the lead in the senior play."

Another says: "As I leave the hospital I try to take some of its cheerful atmosphere, friendly spirit, and its peace into a hurried world. These children have not lost faith in God or man, so why should I?"

2. *From a volunteer at the blood center:* "I never knew so much responsibility lay in this work. After working there a while I realized the important part blood took in our lives and the good work the center is doing. When my required hours were over I was so captivated by this work that I decided to help out as long as I could."

3. *From a volunteer at a neighborhood social club* (for people 65 and over): "We were so pleased with our first visit to Neighborhood House that we looked forward to continuing visits." At the close of their required hours the girls reported: "All in all it has certainly been a gratifying experience. The club members show a marvelous sense of humor, liveliness, and a feeling of comradeship toward one another and toward

[5] Quotation from a letter received from Mrs. Long, January 1954.

the volunteer workers associated with them. We hope to continue coming to many more of the 'gatherings' though it will be some time before we qualify for membership."

Cleveland, Ohio, Teen-Agers in Volunteer Social Work

About eight years ago a course in "Special Sociology" was instituted in the Social Studies curriculum of the John Adams High School in Cleveland, Ohio. The story of it was sent by Mr. John Smetz, teacher of the course. The program is similar to the one in Louisville except that at present it is less extensive and the volunteer work carries a 10-point credit toward graduation. Students must apply for the course and gain permission from their home room teacher.

Each student who enrolls in the class is expected to volunteer for two hours each week in one of the neighborhood social service agencies. They have ten agencies from which to choose. These include a Fresh Air Camp, a Day Nursery, the hospitals, a community center, and four settlement houses, two of which are Negro. The assignment to one of these agencies is arranged and supervised by the Junior Volunteer Committee of the Welfare Federation of Cleveland. The work varies for the teen-agers in different agencies. In the settlement houses they sponsor dramatic groups, sports, and special interest groups; in the nurseries they help to care for the children and to supervise their activities. In the hospitals they serve as corridor hostesses and nurses' aids. This work is well supervised by the agency. Each week the students prepare a written report on their work which is discussed in class.

With the supervision of adults the students plan this work, solve problems, and learn much about human relations. Their reports show that they are happy to do something worthwhile in the community without monetary reward. Many of them continue to do volunteer work in the agencies after they complete the course.

How Baltimore, Maryland, "Enlists the Teens"

This account is unique because the program developed largely through the conviction and persistent hard work of one man, Mr. Harry Bard of Baltimore. The story was first told by Mr. Murray Tuck Bloom in the March, 1953, issue of *The Rotarian* and was later told again in *The Reader's Digest.* Both publications have graciously given permission for this retelling in condensed form.

Mr. Bloom's orginal article in *The Rotarian* was called, "Enlist the Teens" and that is exactly what Mr. Harry Bard did. His conviction that it could and should be done grew out of a number of observations which were disturbing to him. The first was the fact that no "young new faces" were in evidence among the members of organizational committees and boards on which he himself was active. He noticed that the burden of organizational financial drives was carried year after year by the same people with the "same tired faces." He saw that the young people had lots of ideas and energy which were not always used for constructive purposes. He was certain that none of the community organizations were preparing for the future by developing the interest and loyalty of younger people in their work.

These observations led him to the conviction that this situation was unhealthy. He evolved a plan in his own mind to remedy the situation and then proceeded to see what he could do about it.

Mr. Bard's first step was to approach each organization, one at a time, to find out (1) if they were interested in "enlisting the teens" and (2) to find out what volunteer jobs were available which teen-agers might undertake. He made it very clear that he was interested only in jobs that would carry the same kind of responsibility which adults doing the same work would have to assume. He found a satisfactory answer to both queries.

He next approached some high school students. The Senior

Class president spoke for most of his classmates when he said, "We've been waiting a long time for a chance like this. We have to keep reassuring ourselves that we're real people, that we belong, that we amount to something. Everything in us is itching to be up and doing. What high school student wouldn't grab at the chance to do an adult's work and be treated like one!"

The teachers consulted were neither very sure about the idea nor enthusiastic about having to readjust their schedules in order to release interested students one afternoon each week. Many thought that this kind of thing was "out of bounds" for education. After much more patient work the plan was adopted by two high schools in Baltimore.

This is the way the plan works. During the first few weeks of school, leaders from the separate agencies talk about the kinds of work they do, indicating the types of volunteer work that teen-agers might do. Then the interested students visit the agencies to see first-hand what the possible jobs are like. Finally, on the basis of the talks and the visits, each student chooses his work. They are trained by the agency and receive extra class credit for services to the community.

The plan has been in operation nearly four years. The youngsters have helped nearly every agency in Baltimore, from making posters to driving ambulances and helping people in housing projects. The agencies were more than pleased with the quality of the teen-age work. They also discovered that they worked even better in groups.

For example, the Baltimore Safety Council wanted to get a bicycle safety program in operation. Teen-age advice was sought and given toward developing a workable program. As another example, the Citizens' Planning Commission and Housing Association needed a pamphlet to explain its work to the young people of the city. A team of teen-agers went to work, studied the subject thoroughly, and turned out a simple, persuasive, illustrated booklet.

In preparing the article for *The Rotarian,* Mr. Bloom interviewed many parents and teen-agers in order to find out what their reaction to the program was. In relation to parental attitudes he found that "parents are appreciating what their teenagers can do and are themselves being stimulated toward greater interest in the agencies." He found that most of the Baltimore high schools are now "sold" on the program. School vandalism has declined appreciably. With regard to the teen-age point of view Mr. Bloom says, "The three most frequent answers they gave me were: 'It gave me confidence in meeting people'; 'It gave me real responsibility for the first time in my life'; 'I'm getting a lot of experience for a paid job later.' "

Guideposts from This Chapter

IN RELATION TO ADULT ATTITUDES

1. Attitudes are influential and contagious. Discouragement breeds discouragement no matter in what age group we are.
2. Faith in life and in oneself, or the lack of it, reflects in the degree and quality of confidence in others—especially in youth.
3. Teen-age attitudes and behavior cannot be fairly judged apart from the consideration of the attitudes and behavior of adults with whom they must be inescapably associated most of the time.
4. Adult attitudes must be those the teen-agers can trust, and behavior that which they can respect. "Every adult we know influences us in one way or another," so say teen-agers.

IN RELATION TO UNDERSTANDING TEEN-AGERS

Adults must recognize teen-age needs and understand the kind of behavior resulting from their own efforts to meet those needs. Two basic needs are these:

1. Achievement of a sense of personal worth (to be accepted "as he is") and faith in his potentialities.
2. Achievement of independence, interpreted by youth as the right to make decisions and the right to make some mis-

takes from which they may learn. The home is the chief place of conflict about the fulfillment of this need, according to this interpretation.

IN RELATION TO UNDERSTANDING OUR RESPONSIBILITY TO TEEN-AGERS

Teen-agers have no one to depend upon for guidance except adults because they are more experienced than children but less experienced than adults. Teen-agers are in between.

1. They will accept guidance *if* they feel that they can trust us and that we trust them.

IN RELATION TO ACHIEVING ADULT-YOUTH CO-OPERATIVE ACTION IN A COMMUNITY

The achievement of mutual confidence is a process. Its starting point is confidence in the individual self, which slowly and gradually extends outward to the achievement of equal confidence in other selves. In the development of mutual confidence between adult and teen-ager, the process tends to be slower than between adults and adults or between teen-agers and teen-agers, because adolescents are not yet accustomd to the "give and take" process with adults. They need to sense adult confidence in them before they feel free to say what they really think and mutual confidence can result.

The development of adult-youth co-operation in any community follows a definable pattern of gradual growth which varies only in details due to the individuality of each community situation. This pattern is as follows:

1. Adult confidence in teen-agers produces the opportunity for them to show what they can do about any community affairs of interest to them.
2. The result of what teen-agers do with the opportunity initiates a wider range of adult confidence and leads to the discovery of at least some interests held in common with adults.

3. The wider range of adult confidence produces opportunity for more teen-agers to share in the solution of a community problem, or in community activity which does not involve a problem.

4. The possibility of adult-youth mutual confidence and co-operation is seen by more and more within each age group and at the same time it is firmly established between a nucleus of adults and teen-agers who have experienced it to a greater degree.

5. Mutual satisfaction in the new relationship becomes a dynamic incentive for this nucleus to cement the partnership feeling and to find ways to widen the range of co-operative efforts and to widen the extent of mutual confidence between the two age groups in the community.

6. This incentive does widen the range, and a trend is firmly established toward adult-youth mutual confidence, co-operative attitudes and actions.

IN RELATION TO THE METHODS OF DEVELOPING MUTUAL
CONFIDENCE FOR THE GOOD OF THE COMMUNITY

1. The initial move can come either from adults or teen-agers. If from youth, the adults will let them go ahead as far as they can with their own ideas for a solution to a community problem, but will stand by, ready at all times to help, and let the young people know that they are back of them.

2. Adults will give full credit for whatever teen-agers accomplish.

3. Adults will be willing to pick up and carry out constructive teen-age ideas which youth do not have the ability or the authority to effect, crediting them with the ideas.

4. Adults will be willing to share frankly with youth their ideas and opinions—not in the spirit of "We are right," but in an effort to iron out misunderstandings and to arrive at agreements upon which co-operative action can be based.

5. Adults will recognize the role which the school can play in the affairs of the larger community, foster any community interest shown by a student council and the teacher-

advisers related to it, and encourage active interest in the community among members of the student body and the PTA of the school. Education involves social responsibility as well as mastery of academic facts.

6. An unqualified *must* for adults is to be willing to listen to teen-agers at all times and with the same respect they would show to other adults no matter whether they agree or not with their point of view. The freedom of the individual to speak and his right to be heard is one cornerstone of our free society into which young people will soon legally pass. The other cornerstone is responsibility, which brings us to the last guidepost in methods of developing mutual adult-youth confidence for the good of the community. If young people are to develop responsibility as well as freedom, adults must have enough confidence in them to give them an opportunity to experience the meaning of it. One way to do this is to make a place for them within our social service agencies. In doing this:

7. We must make sure that the responsibility offered to them is real, from their point of view, and give them adequate training so that they may gain confidence in meeting the responsibility.

All these guideposts apply equally to establishing mutual confidence and better relationships in the home, with only slight variations to fit the smaller home community. In fact, what happens in the home may have an important bearing on how rapidly adults, outside the home, will accept teen-agers as helpful and co-operative members of an adult controlled community.

TEEN-AGERS AT WORK IN YOUTH ORGANIZATION PROGRAMS

In three of the four stories in Part One of Chapter 2 about communities with a problem, teen-agers with youth group experience were able to take some initiative when adults with whom mutual confidence had developed offered them the opportunity. In the fourth story the young people were discouraged, both about doing anything themselves and about finding adults to help them. The implication is that those with youth group experience are better prepared to know what to do than those without it. They also feel the assurance of some adult confidence which the others lack.

And so Chapter 3 takes a look at (1) types of youth organizations, their adult leadership and financing; (2) the over-all objectives of adult sponsored and guided youth programs; (3) some specific programs in order to see why the young people taking part in them have an opportunity to develop confidence in themselves and in adults, and why they are prepared to work co-operatively with adults in the organization and in the community.

Types of Youth Organizations

The youth organizations mentioned here are those usually referred to in community reports as "youth-serving organizations." This simply means that the youth program is adult sponsored and financed in whole or in part, and that leadership for the program is shared by professionally trained and lay adults. The general organizational policy and specific program objectives are usually controlled by lay people, but they depend in their own thinking and policy making, upon the wider experience of those professionally trained for guidance.

Some of these youth programs, such as the Scouts or the Camp Fire Girls, are exclusively youth membership organizations which include younger boys and girls as well as teenagers. They must depend entirely on adult contributions to supplement the membership fees in order to keep the cost to the boys and girls at a minimum.

Other youth programs such as the YMCA's Hi-Y-Tri-Hi-Y and the YWCA's Y-Teens are an important part of, but still only a part of, the whole organization which also includes younger boys and girls, older youth and adults in different programs from the one designed for the teen-agers. There is, however, an effort to establish some continuity in program planning so that one age group can naturally fit into the next age group. Organizations in this category must also depend heavily on contributions from adults in the community, but the higher adult-membership fees also help to subsidize the low-cost youth program.

Still other organizations, specifically the 4-H Clubs, the Future Farmers of America, and the Future Home Makers of America, are sponsored and financed by the U. S. Department of Agriculture and the U. S. Department of Health, Education, and Welfare, respectively, with no cost to the boys and girls.

All these organizations as well as others like the Junior Red Cross, for example, are national as well as local in organization and membership.

Other constructive youth organizations are sponsored by men and women in the service clubs such as Kiwanis, Rotary, Optimist Clubs; in social service agencies, churches, business organizations, and the like. These are, usually, although not always, sponsored and financed by interested adults in the local community.

Many communities sponsor Youth Councils, the purpose of which is to provide young people with the opportunity to extend their interests and to use their abilities in relation to the affairs of the larger community. Membership in these councils is on the basis of representation from each of the community youth-serving organizations, church groups, and school student council groups. Effort is also often made to include representatives from among the young people who do not belong to any organized youth group. Many communities also sponsor youth centers, which are usually mainly for healthful recreation, but often groups within the total membership of the center develop an active interest in community affairs.

Most high schools make some provision for student government through an elected Student Council and some, as we have already seen, co-operate with community service agencies in developing teen-age social service programs. In one California high school a citizenship training program called "Junior Statesmen" has developed. It has spread quite rapidly to other high schools in the state and to those in a number of adjoining western states.

Many high schools are faced with the problem of sororities and fraternities which must be mentioned among the youth organizations because of the wide acceptance among the boys and girls themselves. They are not sponsored by the schools or by any adult group, as a rule, nor do they have adult guidance or leadership. They spring up because of the teen-age need to belong. Their membership policy is always highly exclusive and it hurts those who are not chosen.

SOME SPECIAL YOUTH PROGRAMS

Some programs do not provide a continuing youth group experience, but many of them contribute greatly to the development of teen-age abilities and prepare them for effective co-operative activity with adults.

Perhaps one of the most outstanding, which has continued annually and grown in scope since 1935, is the American Legion program called Boys State, Boys Nation, and Boys and Girls County Government. The women's auxiliary of the American Legion is developing a similar program for girls in many states. Another is the YMCA "Youth and Government" program. The American Legion also sponsors a nation-wide radio and television program "Youth Wants to Know." This, and similar programs otherwise sponsored, create the opportunity for young people to talk with men and women prominent in local, national, and world affairs.

A number of newspapers sponsor youth forums on subjects of national and world interest. An outstanding program is that of the New York *Herald Tribune,* which sponsors teenagers from twenty or thirty countries. These boys and girls live in American homes for an extended time and go to school with our boys and girls. The visit culminates in a Youth Forum, to which all the New York City schools and those of surrounding environs send delegations. In 1955 similar teenage forums were held in London, Paris, and the Near East. Local young people participated, with a youth panel made up of the foreign delegates who were returning to their homes and some American boys and girls with whom the foreign guests had been living.

THE OBJECTIVES OF YOUTH-SERVING ORGANIZATIONS

All the organizations which fall within this definition, as well as the specific special programs mentioned and many others not mentioned, have one over-all objective in common: to develop good teen-age citizenship now and to prepare young people for the responsible adult citizenship which they must practice in the near future if our country is to remain free and strong.

The effort to fulfill this primary objective is carried on with some specific objectives which each organization attempts to achieve in accordance with the detailed policies and programming ideas of the professional and lay people who sponsor the youth organization. These specific objectives can be stated in general terms like the following:

1. To help each boy and girl achieve a sense of personal worth through discovering his potentialities and through realizing them as far as he is able during his association with the youth program.

2. To provide teen-agers with satisfying membership in a congenial group with an acceptable and purposeful reason for existence. This meets the teen-age need to belong, with a plus value which the high school sororities and fraternities rarely have.

3. To develop an appreciation of ethical standards of behavior and the relationship of spiritual values to the development of good character, responsibility for oneself and others and for the preservation of our free society.

4. To understand the meaning of democratic procedures through the practice of them in their own youth groups and to appreciate how individual freedom is preserved and individual responsibility is developed through such practices. Such opportunity comes not only within the small group but through intergroup activity and through local, regional, and national conferences on a representative basis. These are sponsored by the over-all single organization or in conjunction with one or more similar organizations.

5. To develop a sense of responsibility to their own group and to the organization which makes their group possible.

6. To develop a sense of responsibility to their school community and to the larger community in which they live and finally to the nation and to the world, of which the United States is now inescapably a part.

All the separate objectives are based upon the adult conviction that each individual is free but must be responsible for himself, and also must respect the freedom of others and show that respect through his own individual, influential attitudes and actions in all his relationships in the home, community, nation, and world. This constitutes the essence of good citizenship in our American republic.

The average teen-ager is like the proverbial horse which can be led to the water but will not necessarily drink. Adults can set forth the highest type of objectives, plan the most stimulating of programs—and the teen-agers will have nothing to do with it unless it both captures their interest and meets at least some of their felt needs.

Through concrete illustrations the following pages attempt to show that these objectives, as outlined, appeal to large numbers of boys and girls (even though they themselves might state them in different language), and that the objectives are worked out in practice in a large measure by teen-agers themselves.

We have chosen, as illustrations, to report on some adult sponsored organizations or programs in several citizenship-training categories as follows:

General citizenship training—4-H and YMCA (Hi-Y and Tri-Hi-Y)

Citizenship training in civic affairs—American Legion (Boys State and Boys and Girls County Government); YMCA (Youth and Government); California's Junior Statesmen

Citizenship training in community affairs through youth councils—Madison Youth Council, with emphasis upon structure; San Francisco Youth Association, with emphasis on program; state-wide development of youth councils in Minnesota

Citizenship training in understanding of an experience with our free enterprise system—Junior Achievement

GENERAL CITIZENSHIP TRAINING

The 4-H Club Program

I pledge my Head to clearer thinking
my Heart to greater loyalty
my Hands to larger service, and
my Health to better living, for
my club, my community and my country.

This is the pledge which every member of a 4-H club takes when he or she decides to participate in this national and international program sponsored co-operatively by the United States Department of Agriculture, the land grant colleges, and the county governments of the separate states. The adult objective in promoting this program is to stimulate rural young people to stay on the farms which feed our nation, to find happiness in doing so, and to help the boys and girls to become effective and responsible citizens of the rural communities.

In the last few years "4-H has moved to the cities too. The familiar Head-Heart-Hand-Health program has now proved to have real meaning for both rural youth and his cousin in town. Such widely scattered cities as Detroit, Indianapolis, Portland, and Salem, Oregon, or the metropolitan district of Nassau County, Long Island, New York are dramatic demonstrations. Although still emphasizing the application of new knowledge of home economics and agriculture the 4-H club plan has proved adaptable enough to suit the needs of urban youth. It also develops a greater appreciation of the common problems of rural and urban citizenry."[1]

The 1951 statistical report[2] states that in a typical year there are 2,000,000 4-H Club members between the ages of 10 and 20. These members are organized in 85,000 clubs which elect their own officers, plan and conduct their own programs including social affairs, hold regular meetings, and take part in community improvement.

As many as 250,000 men and women volunteer for that part of the work which interests them most. Some help to organize and advise clubs. These adults may be teachers, ministers, business people, farmers or housewives. Others are "project leaders." For example, a good poultryman will help members interested in a poultry-raising project, a good cook or dressmaker in her specialty, and farmers and livestock men in theirs.

Bulletins, especially designed for 4-H members, are issued

1 Letter from Fern Shipley, Associate Leader 4-H and YMW Program, U. S. Department of Agriculture, October 28, 1953.

2 "Building a Better America Through 4-H," U. S. Department of Agriculture Extension Service. AIB 58, July, 1951, p. 19.

regularly. These keep the young people informed of the most up-to-date developments in homemaking, agriculture and livestock raising. County agents and people from the land grant colleges give additional help through demonstrations of newly developed methods. Members of 4-H have ample guidance from both professional and lay parents and other interested adults.

In any typical year 4-H Club members produce 1,000,000 acres of garden crops, raise 1,000,000 head of livestock and nine times that number of poultry. In homemaking, members preserve at least 10,500,000 quarts of food, prepare 20,000,000 meals, improve nearly 800,000 homes and make over 2,000,000 garments for themselves and their families.

They participate in fire and accident prevention, conduct conservation practices, carry on special health projects; and 240,000 train in home nursing and first aid. An equal number conduct recreational activities, and 415,000 demonstrate improved home and farm practice to others.

"4-H Club work emphasizes the home—in fact, 4-H Club work is home work. . . . By trying new ways of doing practical things in his own home environment and checking results, he makes improvements in well-established home and farm practices that win the approval of the entire family group and this makes for family solidarity. . . . The club member who has the active interest and co-operation of parents naturally accomplishes more; . . . without it the whole project often breaks down."[3]

For example, in 1935 a young man, brought up in 4-H, wanted to raise hybrid corn. "But the old folks in the community were skeptical. Male and female plants—can't be! Pull out the tassels—what a lot of work! Twenty-five per cent increase in yield—not possible! But Dad said 'Go ahead— try it and see if the county agent knows what he is talking about.' Well, everyone around here raises hybrid corn and we are getting 25 to 30 per cent greater yields. And because it is

[3] Miscellaneous Publications, 320, U. S. Department of Agriculture, 1948, p. 6.

a scientific wonder—that pays—95 per cent of all corn raised in America is hybrid."[4]

"A founder of 4-H work refers to it as a 'Back to the Home' movement. And that about tells the story. We learn to do things around the farm and home. We work at home—we study our bulletins at home—we keep our records at home— we have tours to our farm and home. Soon mothers and daughters are working closely together. Business partnerships between fathers and sons often develop.

"Our achievements bring us young folks closer to our fathers and mothers. Parents give us encouragement, and that's what young folks need often.

"A few years back I had just begun my garden project. I had saved my money for the best new varieties of vegetables, got the fertilizer, spaded the ground, and planted the seeds. I had hopes for the best garden in the club, lots of fresh vegetables for our table and visions of canned food for the winter. But there was no rain. And everything was threatened with drought.

" 'That's why farming is a gamble,' said Dad. 'You can't despair, farmers don't. If they did, where would the world get its food? Yes, sir, no one could live on this earth if it were not for agriculture. Let's see if we can't lick the drought.' So there was born courage in my heart and the idea for a simple irrigation system for the garden."[5]

"Our parents help us understand what we do—often suggestions (bulletins and such) are different from the way we have been doing things on our farm. We find it helps to work the

[4] "Building a Better America Through 4-H," p. 10.

[5] "4-H Club Work in the United States of America," p. 21. A booklet prepared for the Economic Co-operation Administration by the National 4-H Club Foundation of America and the Extension Service and Office of Foreign Agricultural Relations of the U. S. Department of Agriculture. This is an attractive, illustrated booklet worked out by a former 4-H Club member, now a leader and a 4-H Club junior leader, for the information of boys and girls abroad. The booklet was published as a result of requests from abroad on the part of many boys and girls who had visited in the homes of 4-H Club members in America.

answers out with our parents. Very soon we will use the suggestion on our whole farm."[6]

"In 1936, Germaine and Germaine made an 8-month intensive study of a typical Missouri baby beef club to try to
discover what, if any, positive character traits developed from
the program. The results of the study yielded the following:
self-reliance, industry and responsibility in doing their own
work; initiative and thrift, judgment, honesty, accuracy in
buying and selling and keeping records; patience, carefulness,
vision, perseverance and 'stick-to-itiveness' in working for a
long-time goal and—most important to our subject—*co-operation and respect for others* in showing one's own animals, in
reaching club goals, and in seeing what others could do."[7]
There is nothing in up-to-date reports which would indicate
any need to modify these findings.

Two other home centered programs for both boys and girls
are The Future Farmers of America and The Future Homemakers of America. These programs develop similar qualities
in the boys and girls and have as large a total membership as
the 4-H clubs. The Future Homemakers of America include
city as well as country boys and girls. Both programs are
sponsored by the United States Department of Health, Education, and Welfare.

*Reasons that the young people active in these programs are
prepared for co-operative activity with adults of any community where they live:*

1. The results of the program illustrate that co-operative
   ability can develop in young people in their own homes.
2. They show a large degree of youth appreciation of parental interest and co-operation.
3. The home is a proving ground for the development of
   good adult-youth relationships because the surroundings
   are intimately familiar, and free from the restraints present

[6] *Ibid.,* p. 14.
[7] U. S. Department of Agriculture, Misc. Publications, No. 320, p. 6.

in more formal social situations. If mutual confidence and a mutually co-operative spirit can develop in the home, as the results of this program show, then we can feel assured that any of the young people active in any of these three programs are "ready" for co-operative undertakings with adults in any community.

4. The program shows also that many of the youthful participants have already developed community interest and are capable of assuming community responsibility.

The YMCA's Hi-Y and Tri-Hi-Y

"The purpose of Hi-Y and Tri-Hi-Y is: To create, maintain, and extend throughout the home, school, and community, high standards of Christian character." This is the statement of purpose which is accepted by each boy or girl, as his or her personal responsibility, when decision is reached to participate in the YMCA program. This purpose has been reviewed periodically by the delegates attending the triennial National Hi-Y-Tri-Hi-Y Congresses during the last twenty years. The only change which has been made is the addition of the word "home" which has always been included in the girls' but not originally in the boys' purpose.

THE ORGANIZATION

The program is available to any boy or girl in high school wherever the YMCA can provide supervision and guidance. In general, it appeals most to those in the junior and senior grades although the younger ones who show interest are not excluded. Provision is made for the younger ones through a similar program called Junior Hi-Y from which they can naturally "graduate" into the more mature Senior Hi-Y.

The organization is local, state, and national. It is also international in Europe and Asia for boys, but not yet to any great extent for girls. In the United States approximately 500,000 boys and girls participate in the program annually.

The local units are organized in clubs of 20 to 30 members

each. They elect their own officers, administer their own club affairs within the framework of general policies existing in the local YMCA unit which sponsors the groups. A professionally trained supervisor and volunteer adults keep the groups supplied with resource materials of all kinds on all subjects in which the members express an interest. The one strict adult requirement is that each club shall have a regular adult adviser who attends all meetings and who is ready to help in all kinds of ways. The clubs choose their own members with no interference from adults and so perpetuate their groups from one year to another because of their interest in and enthusiasm for the program. The free choice of members satisfies the teen-age need to be chosen and to belong. This policy in no way fosters a feeling of exclusiveness because every member knows that any group of eight or ten boys or girls interested in this type of program can request a Hi-Y or Tri-Hi-Y club of their own.

In addition to the small local clubs, councils of representatives of the various separate clubs are organized on a local area, state, or regional basis with a national council as well. These councils have no control over a local club but exist for the purpose of considering the welfare of the organization as a whole and may make recommendations for the improvement of the program or organization. Such a council may even make a recommendation for disciplinary action with regard to a group, which is sometimes taken after the recommendation has been returned to the separate clubs for discussion and voting.

A National Congress composed of elected representatives from all the clubs, convenes every three years. The National Council convenes annually. Both bodies are free to make recommendations to a national adult advisory committee on which some of the officers of the Council and the Congress serve. Other officers serve on other national YMCA committees and on the National Council of YMCA's.

All the clubs together make up the National Hi-Y-Tri-Hi-Y

Fellowship. The president-elect of the 1954 Hi-Y Congress was a boy from Hawaii.

THE PROGRAM

All clubs accept the principle of a "balanced program" consisting of mentally stimulating discussions, speakers, movies, or filmstrips on subjects of their own choosing with no adult restriction placed upon their choice of subject; spiritually challenging discussions and programs on religious subjects and each meeting opened with a brief worship service conducted by the club's elected chaplain; physical activities of their own choosing which are most likely to take the form of group swimming, bowling, roller skating or hikes; social activities which take many forms, the most popular of which is square or round dancing. Each club plans and carries through a service project at least once a year. Many clubs maintain a continuing service program. Some of their favorite projects are parties for children in orphanages, CARE packages, helping in the children's ward of a hospital, and countless other ideas which only the teen-age ingenuity can think up.

ADULT RESPONSIBILITIES

The professionally trained supervisor of each group of local clubs is ready at all times to help with program ideas and is in a position to help the groups develop a thorough-going vocational guidance program, for example. The supervisor helps the boys and girls to set up their officer training conferences, counsels with individuals, trains the advisers and counsels with them on problems arising in their clubs, and works closely with the program's advisory committee. This committee is composed of interested lay men and women and it is not unusual to have teen-age representatives serve with them. This adult interest and help at the local level tends to keep the programs constructive and it is a source of new ideas when the teen-age ones run low.

The National Council of YMCA's sponsors the publication of a monthly news sheet which is available to each club.

Through this publication the various clubs can exchange program ideas. New resource material is announced. Letters from Hi-Y members abroad are often published. In short, it is a major aid in keeping the clubs across the country informed.

An unusual opportunity was afforded all the members because of the existence of this monthly bulletin. In the summer of 1955 an international youth conference was held in Paris as a part of the centennial celebration of the founding of the YMCA in Europe. The theme chosen for the conference was "Living Together" which was broken down into four parts: Living Together with Others, Living Together in the Community, Living Together in the Nation, and Living Together in the World. Discussion guides were published in *Hi-Y Ways* which is the name of the bulletin. All the clubs had the chance to discuss these subjects, summarize their findings which were submitted to the adult conference planning committee, on which the president-elect, Asa Akinka of Honolulu of the 1954 Hi-Y Congress served, together with five other boys who had attended a training conference in Paris during that summer. Four hundred boys and girls from the Hi-Y and Tri-Hi-Y Clubs in this conference participated in person, but hundreds of others shared through using the discussion guides made available in *Hi-Y Ways*.

BRIEF REPORT OF THE 1954 HI-Y-TRI-HI-Y CONGRESS

In order to make the report of the program more concrete, here are the discussion topics which were chosen by the members themselves in the early stages of planning for the Congress. Club members were canvassed for their ideas, and representatives served with adults in planning the over-all program. These topics and some of the ideas growing out of the discussions were as follows:

1. *Boy and Girl Relationships.* They emphasized the importance of common interests, mutual encouragement, self-restraint, co-operation, thoughtfulness, similar ideals, confidence and trust, love of children, and constructive attitudes toward sex.

2. *Family Relationships.* They considered the changes in present-day family life, democracy in the family, how personality develops, the influence of childhood experiences, and how to move toward a future happy family relationship.

3. *Christian Vocations.* They discussed the choice of such vocations, how the choice should work out in practice, and the kinds of possible choices within this category.

4. *Race and Religion.* They reached some conclusions a few of which were these: there is no such thing as a pure race; superiority because of race cannot be shown by any test; prejudices are acquired from others and are not instinctive; Hi-Y and Tri-Hi-Y clubs should work toward the elimination of racial and religious discrimination.

5. *Social Problems.* Some of their conclusions were these: to raise group standards one must be respected in the group; one should be tactful, "be himself," use one's own judgment and not go along blindly with the crowd; teen-agers drink from curiosity, ignorance, lack of attention, rejection, and example of parents and other adults.

6. *World-Mindedness.* They raised the question whether it might not be better for U. S. aid to go through the United Nations instead of directly; agreed on the importance of missions and educational projects; expressed the feeling of need for better schooling about other countries, international problems, world geography; expressed a plea for a wider program of high school exchange students and desired a better understanding of world religions (other than Christianity).[8]

These topics were discussed in twenty-one small groups with several groups discussing the same topic. Each group had an adult co-ordinator.

[8] The full report of the Congress from which these excerpts were taken is available, while they last, from Association Press, 291 Broadway, New York 7, N. Y. The report is called "Forward Together." The complete report contains much of value, by way of lists of resource materials on these topics, for any adult deciding to try his hand with any teen-age group.

CITIZENSHIP TRAINING IN CIVIC AFFAIRS

The American Legion Sponsored Program[9]

The American Legion program has as its slogan, "Building Objective Leadership."

"The American Legion sponsors three top level objective citizenship schools known as Boys State, Boys Nation, and Boys and Girls County Government, to the end that: American Youth may learn that our freedoms cannot be entrusted to others, that each privilege exacts a corresponding obligation and that the ideals and principles of government which have made this country the world's citadel of human liberty, may be understood and treasured as the best defense against dark clouds of hate, persecution and obliteration arrayed against all freedom loving peoples."[10]

BOYS STATE

This program started in Illinois in 1935. Every state in the union now has an annual Boys State in session from the minimum of five days to two weeks at some central point in the state, usually on a college or university campus. The boys are carefully selected from the recommendations of high school principals. They must have outstanding qualities of leadership, character, scholarship, and a service record in the school. They must also be returning to at least one more semester in high school. A corresponding program for girls is gradually being developed by the American Legion Auxiliary.

This is how the program functions. Upon registration each boy is given a government textbook explaining the practice of local and state government. All registrants are divided equally into two parties know as the Nationalists and the Federalists. Each boy may run for any office he may desire. Elections are

[9] Summary of material supplied by Mr. Allan Willard, Director, Americanism Committee, American Legion Headquarters, Indianapolis, Ind.

[10] "Boys State, Boys Nation and Boys and Girls County Government," p. 1, published by National Americanism Commission, Indianapolis, Ind.

held, with campaigns run with great vigor. A member of the State Supreme Court or other high official administers the oath of office. The elected boy then makes appointments pursuant to his office.

The program, while Boys State is in operation, is a balanced blend of instruction in the theory of government and office holding and practice both for elected officials and the ordinary citizen.

On the practice side of the program the Boys State is broken down into city, county, and state government. With each phase of government, citizenship practice is the keynote. For example, practice is given in the operation of the courts, legislative assemblies, public sanitation, public welfare, and so on. Budgets are drawn up, and taxes levied. School boards, superintendent of schools, and road supervisors are featured, each functioning within the laws of the state where Boys State is being held.

On the theory side, special schools of instructions are set up to instruct the candidates for office in the duties of the office of their hopes. After election instruction is given in the operation of government related to each particular office. In addition, schools of general instruction are set up in such subjects as law, civil service, election officials, and peace officials. For example, if a boy wishes to become a lawyer in Boys State, he must go to law school, pass the bar examination, and be licensed. The American Bar Association has offered teams of experts for court demonstrations in Boys States, and many states have taken advantage of the offer.

"Boys State offers opportunities to 18,000 boys annually, to learn the operation of government by operating government. Many states have alumni association members who continue to work for good government, as young adult citizens. Boys States have graduated more than 200,000 outstanding leaders into active civic life where responsible positions of leadership are being assumed."[11]

11 "Boys State, Boys Nation and Boys and Girls County Government," pp. 3-7.

BOYS NATION

Boys Nation, which meet in Washington, D. C., operates on the same general plans as the Boys State except that the participants are more carefully screened for exceptional qualities of character, leadership, and school service. Two outstanding juniors from each of the Boys States are selected. These top leaders with Boys State Experience are given the additional opportunity to learn how the federal government functions.

BOYS AND GIRLS COUNTY GOVERNMENT[12]

This is a community sponsored program in which a committee of high school, county officials, civic, and service groups is formed "to stabilize, co-ordinate, set up, and operate a three-phase program."

The first phase of the program occurs within the communities' high schools. A local attorney or some other qualified person goes to each high school to explain the function and purpose of county government. He also explains the operation of local elections and emphasizes the importance of exercising the right to vote for county officials. All students in the high school are divided into two parties. Candidates for office are selected from the junior class, and elections are held.

The second phase consists of practice in county government for one day. The "junior" officials take the oath of office in the county courthouse. The ceremony is serious and dignified and is attended by county officials, representatives of the press, and other interested adult citizens and young people. During the morning the duties of the respective offices are learned. In the afternoon the junior officials assume their official duties by assisting the adult officials.

"Boys and Girls County Government is paying off in better cleanliness and general upkeep of the county courthouses; greater interest in county affairs in the schools and better

12 "Plan for County Government," in booklet published in 1953 by the American Legion and American Legion Auxiliary, Indianapolis. Ind.

understanding of county officials' duties by all. Adequate text-books on county government are appearing where none existed before. The boys and girls are showing greater interest in the most important right and responsibility of man—that of governing himself."[13]

The YMCA's Youth and Government Program for Hi-Y and Tri-Hi-Y Clubs[14]

"Youth and Government" is a specific aspect of the Hi-Y and Tri-Hi-Y program sponsored by the YMCA. It originated in New York State in 1936. Its emphasis is on the legislative process only. The New York program is called the Albany Assembly. Twenty-nine states now have annual youth legislative assemblies, and four other states are in process of development. Maine has a General Assembly of the United Nations alternating with the State Legislative Assembly. New Hampshire holds a similar one every two years concurrently with the State Youth Legislature. Pennsylvania annually alternates a legislative program for boys with a United Nations program for girls.

From time to time the officers of the state youth legislatures have the opportunity to observe the process at the national level. Well-planned visits to Washington, interviews with Senators and Representatives, and a general conference there, accomplish this purpose.

THE ALBANY ASSEMBLY OF NEW YORK STATE

The Assembly is held in the State Capitol Building in Albany during the first part of December when the legislature is not in session. The chambers can accommodate a maximum of 450 boys and girls. The following procedure is similar in other states. Steps are modified as the peculiar circumstances in each state require.

[13] "Boys State, Boys Nation, and Boys and Girls County Government," p. 11.

[14] Report based on personal experience with the program.

ADVANCE PREPARATION—STEP I

Preparation for the Assembly starts in the separate clubs at least a month in advance of the convening of the youth legislature. The boys and girls take a good look at their communities and at the state as a whole to see what needs improvement and what kinds of legislation may be helpful. Each club draws up at least one bill with the help of a lawyer, a local official, or other qualified adult. This help is with regard only to the form of the prepared bill which must duplicate the form required by the real State Legislature. Adults do not influence the decision with regard to the contents of any bill. The bill must not only be correct in form but also be both timely and debatable.

STEP II

Following the preparation of appropriate bills by the separate clubs, groups of clubs throughout the state meet in a pre-legislative training assembly in a number of designated areas. This has two purposes: it gives a larger number of boys and girls experience similar to that gained in Albany where participation has to be limited by the seating capacity of the Capitol Building chambers; it cuts down the number of bills finally accepted for debate in Albany. Those delegates going to Albany have an opportunity to find out what to expect and how to proceed when they get there because the procedures are identical.

At the first assembly meeting each bill is read by title and assigned to the appropriate committee corresponding to the same one in the real legislature. The bills are thoroughly discussed in committee, revised and voted out, or simply voted out or killed. An adult adviser is on hand, ready to help, if needed. A bill to be considered in committee must be accompanied by adult certification that adequate research has been done concerning the bill's need and value.

The officers always correspond to those of the real state legislature, and the procedures are the same. The only adult who is allowed to speak is the official parliamentarian who does so only when the chairman requests clarification about how to proceed or when a member questions the decision of the presiding officer. Consultation is in private with the officer who then presents the reason for the decision, if he is right or changes it if it was a wrong one.

Bills pass or fail on the basis of interest in the subject, appropriateness as state legislation, and the degree of debatability. This process constitutes a first screening of the bills.

STEP III—THE BILLS COMMITEE

This is a committee of teen-age elected representatives from across the state which, with adult advisers, selects about thirty bills from among all those passing the pre-legislative assemblies. The committee works for a full week end about two weeks in advance of the Albany Assembly. These chosen bills are divided equally between the two houses and are assigned, in advance, to the appropriate committee. They are then printed in an official Bills Book, a copy of which is given to each delegate upon arrival in Albany.

STEP IV—THE ASSEMBLY ITSELF

The Assembly is opened by the chaplain of one or the other of the two houses. The delegates are welcomed by the Governor or his appointed representative. At this first session the bills are read and assigned to committees with all subsequent procedures corresponding to those of both the pre-legislative assemblies and the real legislature, with one exception. At Albany, members of the adult legislature sit in with the committees in order to help by giving desired information and to guide procedures according to the rules of the committee of which he is a member. There is also an adult parliamentarian who helps in other ways, if needed, as is the case in the pre-legislative assemblies.

The following sessions are devoted to debate, conducted in the appropriate house where a bill is passed, killed, or sent back to the committee for revision. It is not uncommon for boys and girls to pass up the one social event—a dance—in order to complete the committee work on a bill needing revision. The entire process takes the best part of three days packed with work and value for the members of this youth legislature.

A sixteen-year-old boy made this comment on his way home: "I always wondered why it takes so long for the legislature to pass a bill but now I see that when everybody can have his say, that takes time. Now I know that when everyone can have his say it's our own fault if anyone puts anything over on us."

Honorable Thomas C. Desmond, for many years a member of the New York Legislature, had this to say:

"Many a lawmaker who first viewed the legislative labors of these youngsters with a superior smile learned to pluck from their sessions ideas which he was glad to use himself. In New York, several proposals adopted by my colleagues in the Senate and the Assembly were pioneered by these youngsters."[15]

This statement was made in 1948. The records of bills proposed or passed by the youth legislatures, compared with those considered or passed by the adult legislature, indicate that Mr. Desmond's statement has become truer as time has passed and as experience has improved the methods of preliminary preparation of the youth delegates.

California's Junior Statesmen[16]

This program originated with a dozen students of Montezuma School in the Santa Cruz mountains of California. The young people had had the good fortune of knowing their teacher, Mr. Ernest Andrew Rogers, very well. His enthusiastic interest in good government, his companionship feeling

[15] "Seedbeds for Leadership," p. 33, *Reader's Digest,* April, 1948.

[16] Condensation of an article called "Stripling Statesmen" by Michael Costello, *The Rotarian,* October, 1953, pp. 12 ff. Condensation by permission.

with his students led to many informal conversations. He always emphasized the idea that "government should not be a mystery to anyone." Convinced of the truth of the idea and "sparked" by the enthusiasm of their teacher, these few boys decided to invite students from the seven high schools near Montezuma to form an organization which would help boys and girls to understand their individual citizenship responsibility. The idea worked and the name they chose was "Junior Statesmen."

"The primary purpose of Junior Statesmen is not to make political leaders, but to persuade young people to participate in public affairs at the grass roots level. The effort is made to help the junior citizens realize: That every voter should understand the political problems he helps to solve by his ballot; that everyone should be able to present his ideas briefly and clearly in public meeting; that he should know the process of government from the precinct to the presidency and that he should know the rules of orderly debate and why it is important to abide by them."

THE ORGANIZATION

Junior Statesmen are organized in local chapters, in the high schools. Each chapter is organized along the lines of municipal government with a mayor who presides at the weekly meetings, a secretary, a treasurer, and a council. The council members act as chairmen of the various committees. The purpose of the meetings is to discuss political and civic problems especially in relation to the local government but also the larger government issues in the news.

To qualify for membership the boys and girls must have a good scholastic record and be active in student affairs. Differences in race, creed, and color are strictly ignored as a basic policy. Members pay dues of 50 cents a week, elect their own officers and two teachers who serve as advisers for a two-year term.

Twice a year Junior Statesmen take part in legislative assemblies similar in purpose and structure to the YMCA "Youth and Government" program. The number of delegates to the assembly depends upon the size of the local chapter.

Twice each year also, the chapters send delegates to regional conventions, the purpose of which is the same as that of the local chapters. These larger meetings provide wider experience in discussion and debate of issues beyond the immediate ones of the local community. In April, 1953, such a convention represented 50,000 boys and girls in 400 high schools up and down the state of California.

The importance of developing the leadership potential has not been overlooked even though the main emphasis is placed on "ordinary citizens." A group of business and professional men in California have set up an endowment fund to send outstanding boys and girls belonging to Junior Statesmen to special summer schools. The girls go to Mills College, and the boys to Montezuma. Noted teachers from the West Coast colleges conduct the courses in constitutional and American government, student government, ethics, public speaking, and English composition. These schools run six weeks. The students for the schools are selected on the basis of scholarship, leadership, personality, and extracurricular activities. The expenses, except transportation, are paid by the foundation. These amount to about $500 per student.

Interest in the idea behind the program is growing. During 1953 Junior Statesmen chapters were organized in Salt Lake City, Utah, in Washington state, and in Oregon and Arizona.

CITIZENSHIP TRAINING IN COMMUNITY AFFAIRS THROUGH YOUTH COUNCILS

A Community Youth Council is one of the most valuable ways for teen-agers to become interested in community affairs and to learn to represent the views of others in order to arrive at a true consensus of opinion about any contemplated action affecting them.

A Community Youth Council which functions well will "produce intelligent volunteers for the community projects, especially those of direct interest to youth and to the whole community in general; it gives the community an additional channel through which to present needed projects and hopefully expect some practical work; it creates and helps to maintain better standards for all neighborhood youth; it acquaints the community officials with the needs and problems of its youth; it furnishes a fund of speakers for public and private agencies for a variety of community uses and projects from finance drives to Halloween parades."[17]

The key to whether a community youth council succeeds or fails lies in knowing how to help it to function well. The "how to" is complicated, depending upon many factors, the most important of which is the kind of adult leadership which is provided. A hardly less important factor revolves around the types of boys and girls holding membership in the council, how they are chosen, and their initial interest in the kinds of things a representative council can do. Still another factor, equally important is the type of program which the council adopts. It must give opportunity for carrying real responsibility, from the teen-agers' point of view and yet not involve projects requiring too long a time for results to show up. The program must be a source of stimulation to the development of new community interests resulting in projects about which the council and the teen-agers it represents can "do something."

Many young people and many adults like the idea of a community youth council. Many councils have been organized and many have failed because of the inability of youth and adults to take these and other factors sufficiently into account. So in spite of the intrinsic value of such a council, adults should not begin to develop better adult-youth community relationships by trying to organize one, except in some unusual community situation. A simple co-operative project, to start, offers a greater chance for a successful council at a later time.

For informational purposes the story of the Madison Youth

[17] "Youth Councils" by Ben Solomon, *Youth Leaders Digest*—Special Issue May, 1955—p. 290.

Council of Madison, Wisconsin, which has been in continuous, successful operation for better than ten years, is given first. The young people, themselves, feel that the structure of the council has had much to do with its continuing success. For this reason the report of this council will emphasize structure rather than program.

The second oldest council in the country is the San Francisco Youth Association. The basic organization of this council is modeled upon the one in Madison and was originally set up in consultation with adults and young people active in the Madison Youth Council. For this reason the report of this council will emphasize program rather than structure.

The third report comes from the State of Minnesota which has systematically gone about establishing a youth council and a corresponding adult council, community by community.[18]

Madison, Wisconsin's Youth Council[18a]

The Madison Youth Council is the oldest in the country. It did not become successful overnight. It was threatened with disintegration more than once in the early stages of growth. Much of the council's success rests in the discovery of what constitutes a sound and workable structure. The purpose of presenting this illustration is to indicate the structure of the Madison Youth Council.

It is a true community council composed of youth representatives from all the high schools and from youth organizations, with a total membership of seventy-five. It has a working relationship with an adult community council. It meets monthly to make plans, discuss, and act on problems which affect the community and the youth of the community. It affords the opportunity for teen-agers of all races, creeds, and

[18] If interest in youth councils has been stimulated, the subject is well dealt with in a special issue of *Youth Leaders Digest* for May, 1955. The issue is called "Youth Councils—Wonderful, Weak or Worthless." Available at 50 cents a copy from Youth Service, Inc., Putnam Valley, New York.

[18a] This report is based on mimeographed material sent by Miss Lillian Nitcher, Staff Adviser to the Council.

Madison Youth Council

This Diagram Shows the structure
of the Council and the interrelationship
with the Adult Advisory Council

colors to work together for the purpose of accomplishing things which affect the youth population of the city as a whole.

Whenever possible the council tries to "farm out" the different problems to its representative groups for action. In this way, many more youth, besides the council members, receive the values of co-operative activity. The only adults who work directly with the council are the staff adviser and five outstanding adults in the community. These adults, by their own recommendation, are deemed to have resigned if they miss three meetings without an excuse. All members of the council come under this same ruling.

The established working relationship with the adult council makes many adult-youth co-operative projects possible. For example, through the combined efforts of the two councils a community center was established, which the youth members feel has done much to cut down the delinquency rate at a time when it was rising in other cities. Also, by means of an adult-youth panel discussion and the combined efforts of the two councils a much needed swimming pool was placed on the books of the city planning commission.

During 1949-50 the Madison Youth Council drew up a brochure called "Steps on Forming a Youth Council" (available from The Madison Youth Council, Madison, Wisconsin). Included in this complete brochure is a section called "The Do's and Don'ts of Forming a Council." Here is the advice this council offers:

The Do's of Forming a Council

1. Make sure that the Youth Council is really representative of ALL interests and major groups.
2. See that the delegates to the council are elected and not appointed.
3. Select a group of prominent, youth-minded citizens as advisers.
4. Make sure that you have a meeting place that is central and that is permanent. (We use the City Council Chambers.)

5. Affiliate with some organization (such as a Welfare Council or Community Chest) that can provide you with the finances necessary for running a Council.

The Don'ts of Forming a Council

1. Don't affiliate for finances with any group which will retain the power to tell you what you can and cannot do. THIS IS ONE OF THE MOST IMPORTANT DON'TS!
2. Don't allow adults to form the council—youth must do it in co-operation with, and with the advice of, adults.
3. AND MOST IMPORTANT—Don't even make an attempt to form a council unless you can have the following:
   a. A regular office, possibly within another office, that is yours. A home is no good as an office. (We have a room in the Community Chest offices that we use.)
   b. A paid part-time staff adviser. (Ours, Miss Lillian Nitcher, is in the Youth Council office and spends one-third of her time on Youth Council work and the other two-thirds with the Welfare Council.)
   c. A stenographer. (The Youth Council stenographer spends about one-half her time in Youth Council work; the other half is spent doing Welfare Council work.)
   d. A meeting place that is central and permanent, and if possible, that will give prestige to the council.
   e. Ample expense money. The Youth Council doesn't need a great deal of money—only enough to cover the salaries of the staff and to pay for stationery, postage, and other miscellaneous items.

The San Francisco Youth Association[19]

The structure of the San Francisco Youth Association is essentially the same as that of the Madison Youth Council. The idea for the Association grew out of a series of Youth Forums called "Youth Speaks for Itself," sponsored by the American Women's Voluntary Services in 1946. The Madison Youth Council was consulted and gave whatever help was needed.

[19] This description is based, by permission, on the following sources: (1) "This Council Really Works" by Sarah Salzer, West Coast Editor of *Seventeen* Magazine, September, 1948; (2) San Francisco Youth Association "Program Report" July 1952-June 30, 1953.

The Youth Association is composed of 171 delegates from the public high schools, 13 Catholic schools, and 8 youth-serving organizations. One unique contribution which this council has made is that it has taken significant steps toward solving the ever-present problem of real representation.

"We do not accept any delegate unless he or she is certified by the school or organization. In this certification the school or organization agrees to provide opportunities for the delegates to report back projects initiated by their delegates. This is the heart of any representative council."[20]

During the first two years the Association was financed by the Columbia Foundation, a private agency. Since that time it has been financed by the Community Chest.

The purpose of the SFYA is "to provide greater opportunity for San Francisco high school young people to concern themselves with the interests of youth in recreation, employment, health, safety, and other community and civic affairs affecting youth, regardless of race, color, creed, religion, or political belief."[21]

The Association has seven regular committees: Civic Affairs, World Affairs, New Citizens, Research and Opinion Polling, Youth Week, Press, Radio and TV. Special committees are appointed from time to time.

The activities of the Association are designed to develop youth's own abilities first of all, but the range of interests and activities are such that opportunities for adult-youth co-opera-tive activity are always present. For example, at least two adult-youth conferences have been held around the problems affecting youth in San Francisco. Adult-youth planning com-mittees set up the conferences. The two groups participated in all the procedures of the conferences as well.

During 1953 an adult-youth project called "Youth Serves the Community" was initiated by the Civic Affairs Committee.[22]

20 Letter from Thomas A. Rowe, Executive Director, San Francisco Youth Association, December 29, 1953.

21 Program Report.

22 Letter from Mr. Rowe, December 29, 1953.

This committee made a survey of youth employment in San Francisco especially in relation to summer jobs. The survey showed that there were many youth who either could not get jobs or did not want them. They developed the idea that there might be a good many volunteer service jobs that youth could do. They then asked the San Francisco Volunteer Bureau to find out how many agencies could use youth volunteers for the summer. Over 200 young people filled such volunteer jobs. They conducted ten weekly television shows that featured the "Volunteer of the Week," usually with the actual persons they worked with, and a "Trip of the Week." A section of the program was called "Just for Fun." This part of the program showed youth doing things in their volunteer job with an agency. This served a dual purpose. It gave the community a chance to see what youth could do to help and also helped to interpret the available community services.

Another example is the annual "New Citizens Day." The young people discovered that there were over a thousand foreign-born students in the Junior and Senior High Schools. Several committee meetings were held with adults interested in new citizens. As a result a permanent New Citizens Committee was set up within the Youth Association structure. Appropriate ceremonies to welcome new citizens are held annually during Youth Week. The ceremonies are sponsored by the Youth Association's New Citizens Committee. Adults and youth participate in the ceremonies.[23]

These illustrations show how a youth council, whose first interest is in developing youth abilities, prepares the young people to see opportunities for adult-youth community projects and to take advantage of the opportunities.

During 1952-53 the various committees reported some interesting projects which did not include adults either in planning or in carrying out of the plans and yet had a good effect on the community. For example, in addition to developing the

[23] Reported in the article in *Seventeen* Magazine, September, 1948.

"Youth Serves the Community" program already described, the *Civic Affairs* Committe planned a "Youth in Government" Day during the annual Youth Week; the *World Affairs* Committe sponsored a conference on the UN on UN Day as well as ceremonies in a public square featuring four high school glee clubs, a band, representatives of seven nationality groups dancing, and student speakers besides. The *Radio-TV* committee planned with the *Press* Committee a series of nineteen radio programs featuring interviews with leading citizens on subjects of the day. A unique feature of this program was that each youth participant wrote a one-minute editorial stating his own position on the subject to be discussed with the guest adult. This was presented before the questioning of the adult began. The *Research and Opinion Polling* Committee interviewed 125 citizens on their opinion of problems in San Francisco on which high school youth should be working. On the basis of the findings, the council began to plan what they could do about some of the suggestions.[24]

In December, 1955, the Committee for Sylvania Television Awards, gave this Youth Association a "Citation for Distinguished Achievement in Creative Television Techniques."[25]

"Hundreds of high school students in San Francisco are engaged in a project aimed at giving Asian Youth groups a view of youth participation in American Community Service." Through the San Francisco Youth Association a traveling exhibit is being assembled for use in Ceylon. The request came from the representative of the Asia Foundation of that country, one of the newly admitted members of the United Nations. Films of two television programs, "Time for Youth" and "Youth Serves the Community" have been sent to youth councils in Ceylon."[26]

[24] San Francisco Youth Association—Program Report, July 1, 1952-June 30, 1953.

[25] Letter from Mr. Rowe, January, 1956, enclosing a reprint of the award.

[26] *New York Times,* December 25, 1955—"Youth Active in San Francisco."

How Minnesota Has Developed the Youth Council Idea[27]

The State of Minnesota has had, for a long time a well-established "Youth Conservation Commission." The work of this commission has been chiefly one of emphasis upon developing ways of preventing youth from getting into trouble with the law and of ways of treatment and rehabilitation after they had run afoul of the law.

During the summer of 1940 an Advisory Council on Children and Youth was established and became a part of the Youth Conservation Commission. During 1948-49 the Advisory Council made a thorough-going study of the status of youth services in Minnesota. As a result of this study the decision was reached to set up similar advisory councils locally for the purpose of finding ways to work through community organizations in order to enrich the life of the community.[28] The decision was also reached that one of these ways was the development of youth councils and youth centers, community by community.

Minnesota defines a youth council as "a broadly representative assembly organized to work with a similar council of adults with objectives of mental, spiritual and physical health, adequate housing, understanding civic problems such as unemployment, recreation, sanitation and social responsibility."[29]

The newsletters and bulletins issued regularly by the Youth Conservation Commission indicate that Minnesota is developing a pattern of community organization in which adults and young people co-operate to solve all the problems which in any way affect the communities' youth, or both adults and youth.

The pattern seems to be to set up two Youth Councils, one

27 This report is based upon a sheaf of newsletters and bulletins called "Minnesota's Youth" sent by Mr. Whittier Day, Chairman-Director of the Minnesota Youth Conservation Commission.

28 Youth Conservation Newsletter, Nov., 1950, Vol. 12, pp. 12ff.

29 "Minnesota Youth," July, 1952, p. 5.

adult and the other composed of young people. The two councils are organized in the same way and are independent of each other except for the common purpose of community betterment.

The "assembly" referred to is a large body of citizens—in one case, adults and in the other, youth. Each respective assembly meets regularly for the discussion of community affairs, makes complaints, and suggests plans for community projects. Each age group assembly has an executive committee which acts upon suggestions growing out of the assembly sessions. The two executive committees act together in any situation which arises affecting either the young people or both age groups.

As adults and youth have gradually learned to work together co-operatively in the smaller community, the desire and opportunity to do so in the larger problems of the state have been created.

In April, 1951, 500 adults and young people met together in a south central adult-youth conference. In 1952 a similar conference was held in the northern area with a larger number of young people participating with the adults. In 1953 conferences were held in both areas. A state-wide Governor's Conference has been held annually in addition to the regional ones, since 1951. Each year has seen an increase in teen-age participation because of their request for wider representation. During the Governor's Conference in 1952 a permanent youth committee composed of one boy and one girl from each of the twenty-eight youth-serving organizations in the state was officially appointed to the Governor's Advisory Council on Children and Youth.[30]

The March, 1953, issue of "Minnesota's Youth" had this note: "Recently appointed members of the Youth Committee will be meeting with the adult members of the council for the first time since they were appointed to membership on the standing committee."

[30] "Minnesota's Youth," July, 1952. pp. 5ff.

These additional facts, not directly connected with any one community youth council are of interest to us because they further support the other experiences which show that once started, adult-youth co-operative efforts grow both as to the numbers who work together and as to the enlarged scope of their activities. In this case a youth council for youth and a corresponding one for adults served as the instrument by which the new opportunities became possible.

Minnesota's conception of the function of a youth council agrees with that of the other two councils described, but with an additional and important purpose of creating a type of organization which not only makes it possible for adults and young people to work together but makes it much simpler as well.

CITIZENSHIP TRAINING IN OUR FREE ENTERPRISE SYSTEM

Junior Achievement[31]

Junior Achievement originated with a group of business men who felt that young people, if interested, had a right to find out for themselves the meaning of the free enterprise system. The program is designed to provide this information and understanding of it by means of personal experience.

They did not know whether or not any teen-agers were interested. This was in 1942. The records kept at the National Headquarters show that between 1942 and 1953 the number of Junior Achievement Companies rose from 108 to over 1500; between 1949 and 1953 the number almost trebled. As of February, 1954, there were 1816 groups. During the school year of 1951-52, 20,000 boys and girls participated in the program. For the year 1953-54 the total number reached 30,000.

31 This account is based on (1) "Don't Give U. S. the Party Line," a booklet published by the National Headquarters, Junior Achievement, Inc., 345 Madison Ave., New York, N. Y., 1952; (2) statistical data supplied by National Headquarters; (3) interview with Mr. Robert Murdock, Vice-President, New York Junior Achievement.

THIS IS HOW IT WORKS

High school students in a typical JA group of a maximum of eighteen members, form a miniature business company. They decide on the services they'll sell or the product they will manufacture. They elect company officers and issue nonlegal, nontransferable stock which they sell at not more than 50 cents a share in order to raise a maximum of $300 needed to run their business. The headquarters for the separate companies in any one place is their bank which is run by standard banking practices. They buy raw materials and tools, keep books, make sales, pay wages, rent, and dividends. In short, they run a big business on a small scale.

This kind of opportunity is open to any boy or girl in high school who shows interest and ability to "make a go" of a company, without regard for race, creed, or color. They stay with Junior Achievement one, two, three, or four years.

Each junior company is sponsored by a business firm or industry. The combined groups, sponsoring the over-all program in any one place, contribute enough to pay the rent for headquarters and buy any large items of machinery which experience shows may be needed by a number of different companies. The junior company pays 10 cents an hour wages to those working on production. The sales people work on commission. The directors of the company are "on salary." All these expenses are paid out of capital stock. Each successful company stays in business for one school year. At the end of this period the books are closed. A report, similar to an industrial annual report is issued to all stockholders, together with a check for the original 50-cent investment plus any dividends accruing from the company operation. A company may organize again for another year to manufacture the same or a different product, but there is no carry-over from one year to the next beyond the experience which the teen-agers gain.

Volunteer adults work along with the companies in four major areas: capitalization, production, sales, and final report.

These adults are members of the company sponsoring the junior one. In each case they work in the same relative capacity in the adult companies. This is standard practice in all JA groups. For example, an adult working in production helps the young people to set up production lines and recommends short cuts to step up efficiency in production costs in order to keep prices down.

As an example of tangible results of this youth activity, one unusual company in New York produced a window-cleaning fluid which users say is better than any currently on the market. The boys and girls were enterprising enough to get an initial order for 4,000 bottles from one of the largest chain "5 and 10 cent" stores. These were delivered and sold, with repeat orders during the school year in which the junior company was in business.

The adults helping with the program are aware of what complete failure may do to the self-confidence of teen-agers. They try to help the young people prevent one. But if, as sometimes happens, a failure does occur, adults help to cushion the "disaster" but at the same time they help the company to understand thoroughly the reasons for the failure.

The adults are also aware that a teen-ager's first work is going to school. Even though many in the production end of the business want to work three or four nights a week, they are not allowed to do so. Sales people work after school and on Saturdays. All others in the company including the officers are restricted to four hours one evening a week. School people appreciate this and are most co-operative in making known the Junior Achievement opportunities to their students.

Values accruing to the members of Junior Achievement companies are these: They learn to appreciate "what it takes" to stay in business by facing the possibility of ultimate failure at all times. They develop ingenuity and creativity in choosing ideas for a business and marketing the product. Responsibility is shown toward the investors who make the business possible. Appreciation of the part investors play in any successful business also develops. They see both sides of the coin, that of management and of labor, and they mature markedly during their year of experience with free enterprise.

This story has been told to emphasize our conviction that to understand and be able to support intelligently the kind of free enterprise system which has made our country strong is a part of the education of teen-agers with respect to American citizenship. This program also holds fast to the value of individual ideas and initiative.

We have indicated that many teen-agers are interested in getting work experience before they have to become self-supporting. This program offers one way in which those who so desire can get work experience but with emphasis upon self-employment and developing a "going concern of their own." It also illustrates another field in which adults can co-operate with teen-agers in helping them to provide for themselves a kind of experience which they feel can be valuable for them. The steady increase in teen-age participation in this program testifies to the fact that it is valuable experience from their point of view.

Conclusions

The programs described in this chapter and many similar ones, speak for themselves in showing why adults are justified in having confidence in the good citizenship of the boys and girls active in such programs; why they have opportunity to develop confidence in themselves and in adults associated with them; and why all are potentially ready for the development of mutual confidence and co-operative activity with adults in any situation and in an organization or community, especially.

All young people do not reach their maximum maturity at the same time or at the same rate. For this reason one should not assume that because a boy or girl is active in any one of these types of organizations he is, by virtue of that activity, ready and interested in wider community experience.

Large numbers, however, of these prepared young people are ready, most of whom have not yet had the opportunity to show what they can do. It is a rare community that does not have at least some of these mature, experienced, and responsible boys and girls who would welcome the chance to use their present abilities and to further develop them by contributing what they can through sharing community responsibility with adults.

All these illustrations show that adults have been both surprised and pleased by teen-age interest, enthusiasm, and ability when the opportunity to help in the community has been offered them. Adults have been even more surprised by the satisfaction which they themselves have experienced while working with young people in the community.

Therefore it is well for adults to give youth a chance and not to be skeptical about them, because all too often we find, with Shakespeare, that

> Our doubts are traitors,
> And make us lose the good we oft might win
> By fearing to attempt.

CHAPTER 4

THREE BOLD EXPERIMENTS IN ADULT-YOUTH CO-OPERATION

The first, of what we have chosen to call bold experiments, is the 1950 Midcentury White House Conference on Children and Youth. This was the first conference on a nation-wide scale which included young people, mostly teen-agers, both in planning the agenda and in free and equal privileges of discussion and voting during the proceedings of the conference.

The second bold experiment is the "Build Freedom with Youth" contest sponsored by the General Federation of Women's Clubs during 1951-52. Prizes totaling $25,000 were offered by the Kroger Company. The inspiration for promoting such a contest grew out of the experience of adults with young people during the White House Conference. The contest was for the purpose of encouraging community women's clubs to find out what co-operative projects the club members could develop with the teen-agers living in their community.

The third bold experiment, started more or less simultaneously with the second, was also a direct result of adult-youth experience during the White House Conference. Two years previous to the conference and in preparation for it the governor of each state was asked to appoint a special Youth Committee to study the youth services presently available and to determine what else was needed. Some states already had an active committee of this type but most did not. At the close of 1951 a Directory was published by the National Midcentury Committee for Children and Youth. This committee was organized to follow up and to encourage the progress made in producing a more active and constructive approach to the problem of meeting the needs of children and youth which was developed during the Conference itself.

In this Directory, each state Youth Committee, or Commission as some were called, stated its proposed program for the year and indicated specifically what portions of it were to be given priority. The states of Indiana, Iowa, Kansas, Michigan, and Wisconsin placed priority on the promotion of "Youth Participation." What these states actually have done about this priority (which means adult-youth participation) constitutes the third bold experiment.

The term "youth participation" needs some explanation, because we have avoided using it. It was and still largely is the term applied to the types of organized youth activity such as we have just described. Oddly enough, this same term is usually applied to the adult-youth activities which we have also been talking about. We have purposely avoided the use of the term in either application because of the confusion which may be caused when a single term is used for kinds of activity which are related but still different.

That the activities, described by the present use of the single term "youth participation," are related is evident. We have seen that those young people who are active in adult sponsored youth programs are, for the most part, the ones most interested in and are now prepared for "youth participation" with adults. The one form of youth activity naturally leads into the other, provided adults are willing that it should do so. We have preferred to call the second kind of youth participation, "adult-youth co-operative activity" so that there could be no question or confusion about what we have meant. From the teen-age point of view, a better term would have been "youth-adult co-operative activity."

We shall describe, in turn, each of these three bold experiments, the White House Conference, the "Build Freedom with Youth" contest, and the programs as each of the five states mentioned have developed them in order to see what we can learn from them in respect to improving adult-youth relationships through co-operative ventures.

THE 1950 MIDCENTURY WHITE HOUSE CONFERENCE

The Midcentury White House Conference on Children and Youth was held in the early part of the winter of 1950. This was one in a traditional series started during the administration of Theodore Roosevelt. One has been held each ten years since that time. The theme of the 1950 conference was "A Healthy Personality for Every Child."

Those responsible for choosing the theme recognized that all teen-agers are interested in the kind of personality they have and in ways of developing it in order to become acceptable members of their own and also of adult society. It seemed to these adults that there were many mature young people, experienced in co-operative thinking and action in their own youth groups who would be interested and able to participate with adults in a conference with this theme. It also seemed appropriate to them that some young people should be included in planning the specific agenda and that larger numbers should have the opportunity to participate in the conference itself.

When the final decision to include the young people was reached, an "Advisory Council on Youth Participation" was set up to plan the agenda. This council was composed of one adult to each three youth members. The young people came from cities and rural areas and represented a variety of racial and religious backgrounds. They also represented cultural, educational, and vocational groups having a national membership of young people between the ages of 14 and 21. Two hundred and fifty high school and college students served on this committee, whose work it was to find out what things were important to youth. An executive committee composed of five young people and five adults directed the work of the committee as a whole.

Among the 5,000 delegates there were more than 400 young people, mostly teen-agers. There were some thirty-five work group topics. In advance of the opening of the conference, each youth and adult delegate chose the one of greatest interest and to which he or she could contribute most. The young people were represented in nearly all the work groups and had full voting privileges in the general assemblies when the final resolutions and recommendations were being considered. Among these resolutions was this one which has a direct bearing on our subject of improving adult-youth relationships through co-operative activity: "No. 5. Youth should be included as full participants in all appropriate community activities."[1]

Although not all adults or all youth were completely happy about their experiences together, this resolution gained the enthusiastic support of the vast majority of both age groups. It seems unmistakably evident that the general feeling of satisfaction gained during this first large-scale experiment was responsible for the determination of the General Federation of Women's Clubs and the five midwest states to try to implement this resolution.

So let's look first at what happened during the "Build Freedom with Youth" Contest, and then at what has happened in the five states.

"BUILD FREEDOM WITH YOUTH"

The Story of Chagrin Falls, Ohio

The top prize of $10,000 in this contest sponsored by the General Federation of Women's Clubs and financed by the Kroger Company went to the Junior Woman's Club of Chagrin Falls, Ohio.

Mrs. Herman Dunfee was active in the project from the beginning and still is, for the project did not stop when the contest closed. She wrote the original, detailed 40-page report which was submitted to the state and finally to the national judging committees. Although she is the mother of several

---

[1] "Children and Youth at the Midcentury," Report on Youth, pp. 5-6. National Organizations, Federal Government, Midcentury White House Conference on Children and Youth.

small children and has a nursery school in addition, she still found time willingly to condense the original report for us. This is her story:

Chagrin Falls, Ohio, is an old-fashioned American town, predominantly residential, with highly cherished traditions, old settler families, and rigid middle western folkways and mores. Although it now serves as a haven for those who commute to their Cleveland businesses, it still remains very much a small town rather than a suburb.

Chagrin Falls Park Allotment is situated about one mile south of our town and is not even within our county lines. It is purely a Negro community, composed of seven hundred and twenty people according to the 1950 census, with one hundred and twenty-two of them on relief in 1951.

Some public-spirited citizens of nearby towns had provided an embryonic Community Center for the Park. Mr. Samuel Carter was the director. Upon consultation with him we found that the Center provided adequate outlets for young children and older people but nothing at all for the teen-agers. We decided that here was something we could do. But before describing what we did let me give you a more vivid picture of Chagrin Falls Park Allotment.

The people of this small place have a few shabby stores of their own but mostly come down our shady, tree-lined streets to shop, to go to the movies, and occasionally to work. Within their own community the churches operate on a rather Victorian doctrine where dancing, card playing, and other harmless social activities are taboo. The school would take pages to describe—with inadequate teaching staff, equipment, heating, and even plumbing! We learned that bootleg whisky can be bought, regardless of the age of the purchaser, and saloons do a seam-bursting business. Sheer survival in the Park presents so many real struggles that little time, patience, or money can be spared for adolescent whims.

The teen-age need to feel needed, valued, and purposeful is as deep and persistent here as it is in every other place. In the worst slums of our cities, it would be difficult to find more primitive social opportunities for teen-agers than here.

The economic picture is equally grim. One hundred and twenty-two people received relief at the time we entered the Kroger contest—but what a minimum figure this seemed when we came to realize the employment problems! No public transportation existed. Despite the thriving taxi duty done by every jalopy in the town, the industries of Cleveland, twenty miles away, could be reached by only a few. Women served as domestics in nearby white communities, but the men's plight was hopeless.

THE PROJECT BEGINS

Mr. Carter and our committee met with a group of teenagers, to discuss their needs. A canteen was their universal request. This they scheduled to open the following week, to function from eight thirty until eleven thirty, on Wednesday and Friday nights. The young people decided upon a fifteen-cent admission fee, with cokes and sandwiches offered at actual cost. Mr. Carter offered the use of an old garage at the rear of the main Center building. This small (21' x 21') building was utterly colorless with its small windows, cement floor, and accumulations of castaways and rubbish. The ability of the youngsters to make do with the available gave us our first shock. On opening night, this shack had been cleaned, festooned with purple and gold crepe paper, and supplied with card tables, folding chairs, checker boards, and any other form of entertainment which could be had for FREE. An old washtub was produced for cooling soft drinks. When we arrived to chaperone, we were confronted by a shabby but spirited picture of festivity. Forty-three teen-agers met to play quiet games, listen to records, and dance.

We encountered opposition in our own community as well as in the Park. Sensing resentment from certain parents, we invited local adults to assist us at chaperoning. To our embarrassment, the youngsters refused to enter, and sent in many comments such as, "What time's the prayer meetin' over?" At the next business meeting, the canteeners themselves selected their favorite mothers to serve with us, and we formed warm relationships with these women, who helped us loyally when bad roads or sick children prevented our attending.

At first, only the original Women's Club committee worked with the canteen members. Later we invited recruits from the club for active participation, and for free baby sitting on the part of those who did not wish to serve at the Center. Our young friends reacted shyly—to say the least—when new white faces appeared. Some remained on guard at the windows to study the situation before summoning the courage to enter. As for our clubwomen, some entered in skillfully and with ease, while for others this crossing of color lines was noticeably strained and trying.

We now feel that ignorance, lethargy, and blind conformity are the main sources of prejudice. Our project did much to destroy these among the clubwomen as well as the youth. Shyness was to be expected, and little by little the boys and girls began to overcome it. We brought ukuleles and songbooks for organized singing, but no songs were known in common. We had to improvise on such themes as "Caledonia" and various boogie and spiritual tunes. We felt pretty antiseptic, armed with our little books of recommended camping songs!

Canteen was a month old before we detected the presence of liquor. There were no fights, no brawls, no scenes, but there was a peculiar milling in and out which we hesitated to probe. The only bathroom on the premises was in the other building, so we had to expect a certain amount of door framing. Finding a boy drinking straight from the flask leaves little to the imagination and, when this occurred, we had to bring up the matter with the young people.

At about the same time one of our mother chaperones encountered three of the boys in a distressing situation with a fourteen-year-old girl who had never before presented any problem to her community. We were not told of this incident by the Negro chaperone. It reached our ears via the elaborate grapevine which exists in such small towns. At first we were discouraged by this inability to communicate. Later, we came to realize that experience had taught these Negro women that well-intentioned white people often fade in the face of such crises. The more protected we could be from such realities the more likely it seemed in their eyes that we would endure. From their point of view it was important that we should. They were trying not to protect themselves, but us.

Mr. Arnold Walker of the Cleveland Urban League gave us excellent and needed advice in many situations. He agreed to inaugurate a program of sex education for the adults in the Park, and set up a program of grooming and hobbies for teenage girls—this to grow gradually into hygienic instructions.

We began to rehabilitate the older problem boys by buttonholing them for greater responsibilities, because they were the known leaders. To control in-the-dark mischief, we issued pass-out slips upon entrance. The young people themselves set up the following as rules: hats off, no profanity, membership tickets to be printed and sold at minimum price, dance floor etiquette, hours, care of property, and control of John Barleycorn. A large chart was printed and posted, so that no one would be in doubt as to boundaries. Committees were formed, and the mischief-making older boys were lured into redecorating the canteen by a promise of newspaper photographs—these to appear in the *Chagrin Valley Herald,* and they did. The older girls selected materials for curtains and carefully chose the chartreuse paint for the walls. Twenty-five young people appeared for duty the night we overhauled the old garage.

Things ran along rather smoothly for a time, but one night a group of forty young people met at the canteen. The scrawny driveway (our only exit) was filled with cars. We noticed a group of Cleveland boys, standing isolated beside the serving table on which stood our "take" for the night—amounting to around $8. Suddenly the boys—AND the money—disappeared. Our older boys raced out to the Cleveland cars, demanding return of the cash. Chaperone husbands were also on hand that night. To their horror, fists flew, and suddenly a gun cut loose —sending a bullet through the shoulder pad of one boy's coat, and sending all into panic.

We met with the canteeners to review the incidents leading up to the gun-play. We learned that gang fights had been long in progress. This was only one of many dangerous interludes! Most of our information came from outraged adults, as the teen-agers abide by the gang codes where tattling is concerned. We learned, to even greater grief, that some of our boys had been picked up for disorderly conduct, resulting from the use of liquor and narcotics that same night. The deputy was in attendance at that meeting, and we had a good look at the attitudes of Park adults! We were told that guns and knives were carried by most of the boys, and the only safe entertainment for adolescents would have to be afternoon functions! The deputy agreed to patrol the grounds. A registry was inaugurated with all guests' names and addresses listed, with the names of sponsors.

Gang play is a normal development in such a community as the Park. These youngsters see themselves barred from rinks, dance halls, playgrounds, and pools in white communities. The hunger for individual prestige, usually vented through sports, arts, crafts remains unsatisfied. Store-bought securities are limited too. The one real opportunity for belonging is in the gang—with top rating for the pluckiest, toughest behavior.

To our delight, we proved that this desire for belonging can be rechanneled. Their money, their ideas, their elbow grease went into their canteen. The project was executed by raw recruits on all sides. These efforts were materially rewarded by the top prize of $10,000. Spiritual rewards cannot be measured.

The money will soon have been spent on a lovely wing on the Center Building—to house projects which will support this movement in an extended program for many years to come. Perhaps in later years our young people will be chaperoning their children, and remember the potbellied stoves they stoked, the ice and water they hauled over impassable roads, the deep breaths that had to be drawn before entering the "white man's bank" with their meager funds. Years will pass before our Center can compare with those we visited with our young people— Karamu, Friendly Inn, Alta House in Cleveland where we studied, firsthand, and learned through exchange visits between Cleveland and the Park.

But there is no question in our minds that the way has been cleared in the direction of greater adult-youth understanding.

THE AFTERMATH

In the beginning the canteen seemed like "kid stuff" to these boys and girls. . . . Today they are working closely with Cleveland's interracial cultural arts center Karamu House, learning much, exchanging visits, and making field trips. Art and hobby classes have been started and talent shows staged. . . .

The members of the Chagrin Falls Junior Women's Club, without any sense of superiority or of do-good sentimentality, patiently laid the groundwork . . . destroying color barriers and overcoming mutual shyness.

Their efforts have been rewarded by the progress of the young people who, working with the club members and with each other, have learned to be active, responsible citizens. Four of the boys and girls from Chagrin Falls Park Allotment were sent to the Minneapolis convention of General Federation of Women's Clubs—at which the prizes for the contests were awarded.

The Story of Clarkston, Washington

This story is a condensation of the original report submitted by six federated Women's Clubs to the National Judging Committee of the "Build Freedom with Youth" contest. This effort captured the second national prize of $3,000 in the contest. Mrs. Melvin Warfield was contest chairman. We are indebted to her for the loan of the original report upon which this condensation is based.

Clarkston is situated in the southeastern corner of the state of Washington where the historic Lewis and Clark Trail crosses the confluence of the Snake with the Clearwater River as it flows toward the Columbia. It is a town of about one square mile within its city limits. It has about 10,000 population including the suburbs but only 5,000 within the city limits where the adult-youth projects took place.

About 1,000 boys and girls between the ages of 12 and 21 live here and go to school in the one Senior High School, one Junior High School, and the three elementary and one parochial school. There are seventeen churches representing nearly every denomination, one library, one airport, three city parks, one swimming beach along the Snake River, and one hospital besides the general store and businesses which benefit Clarkston youth.

Clarkston's economic resources include dairying, poultry and stock raising, soft fruits and vegetables, wheat and pea farming. There are two meat packing and processing plants, some lumbering and milling, and a box factory. The town is in a valley surrounded by towering hills which give it protection from harsh winters. Because of this situation the district is often called "The Banana Belt."

Across the river is Lewiston, Idaho, a city of some 72,000 people. It is more industrialized with greater facilities for work and shopping. As a result, Clarkston remains more rural in character and is less developed industrially than many places with equal or less population. This closeness to Lewiston with its greater work opportunities not generally available to high school boys and girls has much to do with the way in which the first adult-youth project developed. This was a Youth Employment Agency, but no one knew at the outset that this was to be the first one, even though many boys and girls had expressed the desire to work in vacation time for several years previous. Nothing had ever been done about it.

HOW THE PROJECTS GOT STARTED

The six women's clubs are all study clubs with a total membership of 132. In May, 1951, each club elected a representative to a committee to plan projects. Fourteen student leaders were selected from the ninth grade to meet with the adults to explore the possibilities for doing something together. The youth representatives were chosen because they had taken part in a panel discussion on youth problems at a PTA meeting and so had done some thinking about community youth needs.

A boy suggested that a survey be made of available summer jobs, and a girl suggested that the first project be a vacation employment office. So this was decided upon, and two girls volunteered to run the office on a commission basis. The development of the summer work program produced the same satisfaction to the young people as did the similar one in Iowa City, Iowa. The difference in the two programs is that in Iowa City the adults took the initiative in offering help to the boys and girls, while in Clarkston the teen-agers suggested that adults work out a program with them. Because of this difference the Clarkston program developed one step at a time in contrast to the advanced thinking and preparation which the adults in Iowa City had done before the teen-agers were approached with the idea. In both cases the final program adopted was the result of co-operation, and both programs are permanent.

WHAT THEY DID NEXT

The PTA was in trouble because of low attendance due to a number of factors. Some of the teachers could not get to the meetings until they were half over, children who had taken part in a program had to be cared for until the close of a meeting, and the fathers could never attend meetings in the afternoon. The president of the PTA approached the young people on the planning committee to see if they had any ideas. As a result the committee agreed that this would be their next project.

The meeting time was changed to evening at 7:30. The young people did the baby sitting for those who did not want to bring their children along. For those who did, the young people set up a nursery for the smaller ones and a program for the older children. The young people received $1 per evening for the service. The PTA membership increased by thirty families, and attendance jumped in one season from 25 under the afternoon meeting system to 125 at each meeting under the new system.

EASTER CLEAN-UP AND MAPPING OF "EYESORES" IN CLARKSTON

At the August, 1951, discussion meeting the committee explored further and came up with the idea that Clarkston could stand some cleaning up. Streets were assigned to the fourteen young people on the committee and about twenty more whom they had brought in. Sectional maps of the city were made. Sanitary laws were looked up in order for the teen-agers to know whether or not they were being violated. The city officials tended to think this was not youth's business and refused to let the youngsters look up the laws. An adult then went to the sanitation department, explained what it was the young people were trying to do and the co-operation of the department was obtained. Property owners were not very co-operative either. Many lay in wait for youthful inspection teams, ready to tell them not to dare set foot on their property. Gradually the dignity and sincerity with which they went about their work convinced people that youth meant business. The young people made small maps of where they had been and what conditions they found, as their inspection job progressed. The former city engineer agreed to make a large map of the city. When the inspection job was completed, all the information they had put on their small sectional maps was transferred to the large one.

The large map and a report was presented to the City Council. The lawmakers took this piece of work seriously. They had already observed that people had begun to clean up their property *before* the inspection team got to their neighborhood.

They also realized that the young people were discovering flagrant adult disregard for the sanitary laws. This they realized was no example to set for youthful citizens. As a result the Clarkston City Council ordered the city attorney to interview all people who were violating the sanitary laws either through ignorance or willfulness.

At the time this project was going on, the young people felt that they should have some representation on the City Council. Two second-year high school students were elected. The Mayor and the Council had become interested in the efforts to make Clarkston a better place to live in and welcomed the young people. A little later these two young persons were asked to serve also on the Adult City Planning Commission appointed to study future plans for the town. As a direct result of the young Council members' serving on this commission, the high school social science class was asked to take a census of children in Clarkston. This was to be used to help determine the need for new schools and possible centers of population in which to locate them.

THE ADULT-YOUTH PLANNING COMMITTEE
FINDS SOMETHING ELSE TO DO

The hospital was greatly overcrowded and there was an unpaid mortgage of $3,000 which had to be paid before federal aid could be had for the much needed expansion of space and services. The planning committee decided on a Flash Drive for the hospital mortgage. When the plan was proposed, many of the parents objected to the young people's being out on the streets after dark. Others thought that the idea was good but they were tired of money raising and didn't want to do any more work. The teen-agers proposed that adults drive them to the doors of the various houses. This scheme was worked out. The young people and their adult drivers all met at the high school. A group of boys and girls were assigned to each driver, who was responsible for keeping them with him or her and for returning them safely to their homes.

While the plan was in the discussion stage, an adult asked

the young people if they thought prizes should be offered. Their quick and unanimous response was "No, the money isn't for us, it's for the hospital." And for the hospital it was, $2,500 of it raised in one night, because adults and young people worked out a scheme whereby adult tiredness could be coddled and youthful energy used, to good advantage. Fifty-seven adults took 110 young people. The work was done in two hours, and the remaining $500 was raised a few evenings later by a smaller group.

A MORE WIDESPREAD YOUTH PARTICIPATION PROGRAM
TAKES SHAPE

By November, 1951, the planning committee again began looking for something else to do. At this meeting the representatives to the City Council made their report. After some discussion one of the girls suggested that they form a Youth City Council. A boy said, "That sounds like a wonderful idea to me because we won't have to put up with all the gripers the City Council has to put up with, and we can plan the things we're interested in doing."

After discussion they decided that each grade, 7 through 12 inclusive, in the Junior and Senior High Schools should be represented by two girls and two boys, elected by written nomination, observing the same eligibility rules that are required for school activities and holding school offices. This means that citizenship behavior as well as scholastic standing must be average or above.

The highest eight, four boys and four girls in each room, were asked if they would serve if elected and assume the necessary responsibilities. Their names were then placed on the ballot. The highest two boys and two girls became regular council members and joined with the youth members of the planning committee to constitute the first Youth City Council of Clarkston. The third highest boy and girl were alternates in case of illness of any of the regular members. One Junior High School and one Senior High School teacher were chosen to advise the Council along with the youth president of the Planning Committee and Mrs. Melvin Warfield, the contest chairman.

Officers were elected to correspond to the officers of the City Council. The group of 24 regular members, with alternates replacing or filling in when necessary, was organized on December 10, 1951. Committees corresponded to the City Council committees and consisted of Park, Street, Ordinance, Auditing, Health and Sanitation, Lights and Water, and Fire. The original planning committee voted to stand by the Council for the future and give whatever help they wanted.

The balance of the projects were all initiated by this newly formed Youth City Council[2] and then carried through with the co-operation of adults.

The Story of Fulton, Mississippi

The co-operative effort in which nearly all of Fulton's less than 1500 people participated captured the third national prize of $2,000 in the "Build Freedom with Youth" Contest. Mrs. W. L. Orr, with the permission of the Fulton Civic Club, loaned us the original scrapbook and report submitted to the national judges, on which this report is based.

THE SETTING

Fulton is a small hilltop town built around a court square. The original land grants date back to the Itawombo Indians for whom the county is named. Itawombo means Big Bench. Fulton has been the county seat since 1826. The people are about 95 per cent white Anglo Saxon and the balance Negro.

A county agricultural high school was built in 1922, and a Junior College was established in 1948. The increase in educational opportunities improved agricultural methods and a corresponding improvement in the size and quality of crops fol-

[2] As of January 1954, this Council was still alert and constantly looking for ways to further adult-youth activities. They were making progress toward raising money for a recreation center which was being planned by adults and youth. When the center finally becomes an actuality, it will be used by both age groups.

lowed. The chief source of income in Fulton comes from the broiler houses. These are buildings where chicken broilers are raised for the market.

EVERYONE GOES TO WORK ON CO-OPERATIVE PROJECTS

The people of all ages, white and Negro working together, found literally 103 different things to do. At the close of the contest the Mayor of Fulton said, in part, "Not only the civic improvement has been worth while but the training and responsibility given to youth will be of untold value as they take their places as citizens of the future. The co-operation, desire for better living, and the harmony while working together is certain to create a more prosperous and better place to live."[3] One of the teen-agers who attended the convention in Minneapolis where the prizes were awarded said, before the whole convention, "We had no idea how much fun grown-ups were until we started to work with them."[4]

A CHICKEN HATCHERY IS BROUGHT TO FULTON

From the point of view of the general economic improvement this project is considered of top importance. There were already many broiler houses on a paying basis in Fulton, many of which were owned and operated by young people. When a big hatchery company was looking for a desirable location, adults and young people interested in broiler houses went to work. The young people made a map showing the capacity and location of each broiler house. Adults and youth armed with the map attended a meeting where the decision was made to locate in Fulton, mostly on the basis of the concrete information provided by the adults and young people working together to influence the company to come to Fulton.

A SUMMER LIBRARY IS ESTABLISHED

The Fulton Civic Club had organized a small library for younger children each summer for many years, there being no public library in the town. The need for one was felt, so the

[3] Letter from the Mayor, Feb. 4, 1952, Fulton Civic Club Scrapbook.
[4] Reprint of Contest Report, General Federation of Women's Clubs.

adults and young people went to work on this too.

To find a place was the first big problem. Wooden buildings were being torn down in the business district, and there was a town ordinance forbidding the construction of others of wood and making major repairs on those left standing. They finally got special permission to use a small room in a storage building, provided they would clean it up.

Adults and twelve boys and girls scrubbed. Eight boys and girls painted. Tables and chairs were donated. From the State Library Commission 430 books were procured, and the Fulton Civic Club procured 100 more. Fifteen boys and girls with adults unpacked the books, catalogued them and placed them on the newly co-operatively constructed shelves. A corps of twenty-eight boys and girls served in shifts with one adult as librarian. There was no money to hire one. They served all summer long, the three afternoons a week when the library was open. The library was so well patronized that "we feel that this project may well lead to a permanent library for Fulton."

Other projects included "cleanup—fixup—paintup" campaigns which included all property owners; planting an "avenue of trees" along the Fulton portion of the main highway connecting Memphis, Tennessee, and Birmingham, Alabama, as a memorial to the young men who died in World War II and in Korea. With the co-operation of the landscaping engineer of the State Highway Department, boys of the Future Farmers of America dug the trees from the forest and transplanted them. Many of these boys graded and landscaped the court square; a new recreation park was hewed out of virgin land in the colored section of town and when it was officially opened, a community barbecue was held with well over two hundred people in attendance. Merchants of the town donated hams and watermelons, and the girls of the town baked enough pies and cakes for all.

HOW PROJECTS WERE DETERMINED

An adult steering committee, consisting of a chairman, a cochairman and three other members of the Fulton Civic Club, was appointed. They organized a Youth Survey committee whose job it was to poll youth opinion about possible projects for the good of the community as a whole. The adult committee did the same among the adults. A mass meeting of youth was held in the Junior College Auditorium to discuss the various projects suggested. A long list was agreed upon to which others were added from time to time, totaling 103 undertaken and completed during the single year of the contest.

A co-ordinating council was set up to check on the progress of the separate projects and to lend financial aid and other assistance. The Council consisted of the Civic Club steering committee and one representative from each of the groups. youth and adult, who were interested in participating in the all-community project of improving conditions in Fulton. Nine youth groups and eleven adult groups started with the project and stayed with it. Three other youth groups and two adult groups joined in later. Each group chose one or two specific projects from the list. Each was carried out by adults and youth together regardless of whether the sponsoring group was adult or youth.

More Guideposts

The value of this contest lies in the fact that community adult-youth co-operation was a new experience in each of the thousands of projects developed in each state, 3,000 of which reached the national judging committee. From these we can find some guideposts as to (1) the basis for a first co-operative project, (2) methods for it, and (3) the meaning of true co-operation.

THE BASIS FOR A FIRST PROJECT

Guidepost 1. Any adult-youth co-operative project which can reasonably be expected to succeed must be within the range of teen-age interests and their own recognized abilities. This is because interest constitutes the educational and psychological principle called "readiness" which means a feeling of wanting to learn or to do accompanied by a feeling of being able to learn or to do. For teen-agers, interest is the incentive and is the source of confidence in tackling something new. This is also true of adults, but teen-agers have had less time than adults to develop a wide range of interests and less experience in doing something about them. It is for this reason that teen-age, rather than adult, interest should be the basis for starting a new experimental community co-operative project.

METHODS FOR A FIRST PROJECT

Guidepost 2. Whenever adults see a youth need about which the boys and girls can do nothing by themselves—that need can be better met, with more satisfaction to the young people, if adults work *with* rather than *for* them.

The adult temptation is always to do for, especially in a situation as desperate for the boys and girls of a different race and low economic status as those in the Chagrin Falls Allotment. The women felt the temptation as did those in Iowa City. In both cases the temptation was resisted, and the projects succeeded. To do *for* may bring quicker, tangible results but anything adults do should be in the best interests of the boys and girls. By working *with* them, they grow in self-confidence by helping themselves, and so take a step forward toward their conscious or unconscious goal of independence. They also experience the meaning of co-operation, which is the foundation of free society.

Guidepost 3. Adults and teen-agers should explore the possibilities together of what the project shall be and choose, by mutual agreement, where to start.

Two of the prize-winning projects illustrate the exploratory method but show two different ways of going about it.

In Clarkston, the exploration was conducted by an adult-youth committee which chose one project at a time. It was then carried out by them and others of both age groups. In Fulton, the exploration was done by separate committees of adults and youth. The results were put together, and a workable list was agreed to by all interested in the co-operative experiment. From this list groups of adults and youth chose one or more projects of special interest to them and carried them through together.

The Clarkston way is probably more practical in a large place and the Fulton way more practical in a small one. The Fulton way would, however, be completely practical in a neighborhood-by-neighborhood development of adult-youth co-operation in a large city.

THE MEANING OF CO-OPERATION

Dr. Max Wolff, Community Consultant, Columbia University, at the time of the contest, and chairman of the national judging committee said, about the 3,000 projects which reached the final judging: "All these projects fell into three classifications. Although all were called co-operation only one type was truly so."[5] The following three types of situations illustrate what he meant:

Type I—to be avoided. Adults come together by themselves to consult about a problem involving youth or about the possibility of a co-operative project. The adults reach conclusions and make decisions. Then they invite a group of young people to a meeting. They tell them of their decisions and their plans and then say, "Don't you think this is a good solution or a good idea? Will you help us?" The young people are really on the spot. They hesitate to disagree or to make suggestions especially to adults whom they do not know. The result is that they agree halfheartedly to go along with the adult plans. They have no real enthusiasm with which to spark their own efforts or to kindle a flame for activity in other teen-agers because they have had no say in what they are asked to do.

This is not the sharing of ideas which all co-operative thinking must be. Some success may be realized in the particular undertaking, but no genuine give-and-take relationship has been established; consequently, there is no mutual confidence

[5] From an interview with Dr. Wolff.

and no incentive to continue the relationship or look for other things to do. It is more than likely that word would get around via the teen-age grapevine, "Don't accept any invitation to attend a meeting of those adults!"

Type II—to be avoided. A group of adults and young people meet together for the express purpose of pooling ideas about some kind of co-operative action for any one of a number of possible reasons. The adults discuss their own ideas, ignoring the young people. As an afterthought, or intermittently, some adult may say, "Let's hear what the young people have to say." Under these circumstances the young people are thrown off their guard. The chances are they have been busy with their own thoughts and therefore slow in being able to formulate any ideas at all. Because of their slowness, or hesitancy, in speaking up, the adults go right on talking about their own ideas again. They arrive at conclusions, dismiss the meeting and honestly think that they have given the boys and girls a chance to have their say when in reality they have not created that kind of atmosphere which would make it easy for youth to speak up.

This is not co-operative thinking—it is unilateral. Failure to establish a permissive atmosphere is very often due to lack of adult "know how" because of little or no experience with young people in groups, but it can be and sometimes has been because some adults feel that "the thing to do" is to include youth in their planning group without genuinely caring what the views of the young people are.

Any suspicion of a lack of adult sincerity or failure to make the teen-agers feel that their ideas are wanted, whether intentional or unintentional, leaves a young person cold to any ideas which might involve them. This second type of procedure almost guarantees failure from the start.

Type III—to be considered most carefully and cultivated. Adults and youth sit down together. Effort is made to talk about ordinary things while waiting for the meeting to begin. The majority of the adults genuinely want to hear youth's side of the question or to benefit from their ideas. The teen-agers sniff the atmosphere.

The adult chairman may say something like this: We have an idea that we would like your opinion about (and he briefly outlines the idea)—or, we have a situation here which needs correction (and he outlines the situation as the adults see it). This situation affects you too, so we have come together that we may put our ideas together and see where we come out. How do you see the situation, or (if it's an idea) what do you think of the idea?

The adults may have some definite ideas, but in order to make the young people feel free, they offer them the first opportunity to speak—and give them time to do so. The time may seem endless but it is worth the wait to allow a boy or girl to "break the ice." Before too long, a give-and-take discussion begins. Nothing much may be accomplished at any first meeting, but a cordial relationship has been established to a degree sufficient to allow the group to reach some co-operative decision about what the next step should be.

Basically this kind of process involves a genuine desire to know what the young people think, a sincere invitation to them to express their views, adult courtesy in giving them all the time they need both to get started and to say what they want to say, and the adult wisdom which shows appreciation of the fact that teen-agers are generally unaccustomed to have adults ask what their views are. All these adult attitudes added together tend to make the younger people in the group feel at ease and develop their confidence in the fundamental honesty of the adults, and, though we may not be consciously aware of it, that democratic co-operative process which can't be stopped because of its own dynamic power to produce better relationships, is set in motion.

It is just as simple as that.

So much for the communities. Let's take a look now at what those five states which set a priority on the development of adult-youth participation have been doing.

STATE-WIDE ADULT-YOUTH CO-OPERATIVE PROGRAMS

Report from Indiana

Indiana has a State Council for Children and Youth appointed by the Governor in 1949. The executive director is Miss Mildred French. We are indebted to her for this report. Through the activities of the Council, local, regional, and county committees on children and youth are being set up.

During 1953 the Council sponsored a series of thirteen TV panel discussions on parent education. At the time of this report the current one was called "Youth Looks at Safety." The panel was composed of high school students who presented their views on how the traffic problem looked to them. The program opened with a dramatic presentation of one special problem causing traffic accidents—for example, mechanical trouble. Each program followed the same pattern discussing a single cause of traffic accidents, one at a time. The purpose of the program was to increase traffic safety for all age groups and to show the cause of each type of traffic accident.

In the fall of 1953-54 youth representatives, from all over the state met to form a State Youth Council. The purpose of this Council is "to work co-operatively with the Senior Council in studying the problems of children and youth in Indiana." The two Councils together chose a specific project for their first year of work. This was "to develop a questionnaire that will form a basis for adult-youth discussion across the state around the subject 'How Can Adults and Youth Work Together?' " The Councils hope that through wide discussion the pitfalls of the past and present can be discovered which have caused both age groups to feel that it is quite impossible to work together.

Miss French sums up her report this way: "It would seem to me, offhand, that Indiana is for the co-operative spirit that is going on in adult-youth relationships. In several medium-sized cities youth have become a part of the Mayor's planning committee. Reports are coming in from all over the state of 'rapid fire' youth-adult planning committees working away from 'vandalism.' Reports are coming in of youth taking part in presenting panels to adult audiences around the subject of youth's own ideas of what can be expected of them." Miss French's closing paragraph should be framed and hung conspicuously so that we may not forget the importance of it. She says, "Perhaps the most interesting thing which has developed from this adult-youth participation in Indiana has been the advancement of these ideas:

1. *Young people do not want to be left alone.*
2. *Young people seek guidance from adults.*
3. *Community projects, to be successful, must be given guidance from adult groups.*
4. *This adult guidance must be given in a way which is acceptable to youth.*

Report from Iowa

Iowa has a State Commission on Children and Youth. It was organized privately in 1948 and made official by appointment by the Governor in 1949. We are indebted to Miss Esther Immer, its executive secretary, for this report from Iowa. The Commission made some surveys to determine recreational facilities, family life practices, youth employment, and other subjects related to youth affairs which have led to some projects in which adults and youth are participating.

The surveys made in local communities to determine the recreational and other needs of youth, originated in one way or another with the young people, mostly through the help of local women's clubs. In some instances adults organized and determined the needs of children and youth first, and then brought in the young people to participate in determining the best ways of meeting those needs. Concrete results showed up in the development of summer recreation programs, swimming lessons for communities which had had none before, organization of library facilities including story hours for children. Other projects were initiated by high school students who were asked to write essays on what they thought the needs of the community were. The ideas in these essays were tabulated, and a committee of young people and adults went to work (1) to see which needs should be tackled first, and (2) to decide on ways to do something about them. Family Life Panel Discussions were held in many communities to find out what some of the family problems were and to discover what adults and youth could do about them together. Here are five specific examples of community projects which developed because of the encouragement and work of this State Commission.

FUN FOR THE FAMILY

In a town of 300, which did not have a local newspaper, publicity about a project to find out what the young people felt they needed was carried on by the school newspaper. This was written, edited, mimeographed, and distributed by the young people themselves. They had to scratch to find enough paper to mimeograph the news for distribution in the community. The churches co-operated by contributing some paper. Other organizations did likewise. The decision was reached that the priority need of the young people was to learn square and social dancing. They raised enough money to hire a teacher from out of town. The result proved to be a family affair. Almost the whole community turned out for the lessons.

HOW TO FIND OUT WHAT A TOWN NEEDS

In a town of less than one thousand, high school students wrote essays pointing out that they needed recreational facilities, a library, safety training in driving, and a youth fund so that dances could be continued. A joint committee of adults and youth went to work. The tangible results of their joint efforts were a public park, a skating rink with indoor facilities for floor, flower, art and style shows, many of which are being currently held. The young people themselves put across a program of better practices for bicycle riders. The young people feel so much was accomplished that they are now organizing to help adults complete plans for a library and a swimming pool.

NEED A BETTER SCHOOL? YOUTH AND ADULTS GET ONE

In a city of 7,000, youth and adults decided that the elementary school was completely inadequate. The community had voted a school building tax, but inflation had cut the value of the funds making the tax inadequate. Young people and adults in organized committees enlisted volunteers to raise extra money, but this money too suffered from inflation and the school could not be built. The young people co-operated in circulating a petition for another school bond issue. On election day they worked "to get out the vote." The final result was the much needed elementary school and a much needed community auditorium for concerts and public meetings in addition.

NOT ALL YOUTH WANT TO BE ROWDIES

In one city a Family Life Institute was held because of a lot of troublesome youth behavior which bothered the adults. The subject was "Standards of Behavior for Young People."

The high school auditorium was jammed with young people and adults. Young speaker after young speaker said that this was the first time they had ever been allowed to be heard and to help to find solutions to problems which bothered them too. They said "a lot of teen-agers do not like being 'lumped with the minority' who make life miserable for everybody." They said they felt that the majority of teen-agers want to be co-operative in their behavior for the best good of everybody.

This meeting of adults and youth was supposed to close at 10:00 P.M. When the chairman put the question of adjournment, adults and youth alike wanted to continue and did so for two hours longer. This first meeting led to some agreements between adults and youth about what constituted acceptable youth behavior in this particular city.

SOMETHING TO FRAME FROM IOWA

1. *An idea for needed action can come either from an adult group or a youth group, and a satisfactory solution comes only when the two groups plan the action to be taken and carry out the plan together.*

2. *A co-operative adult-youth project can help youth to become experienced enough and mature enough to go ahead "on their own."*[6]

Report from Kansas

The Kansas Council for Children and Youth was organized in 1942. It is a voluntary organization but was recognized by the Governor in 1949 and again in 1951. This Council included youth in its membership prior to 1950. Mr. B. W. Tucker is executive secretary and it is to him that we are indebted for this report.

This is a report which gives us a picture of several youth Council members at work. A Junior High School girl served on the Council committee responsible for policy making, co-ordinating, and publicity. She gave many talks about the White House Conference to which she was one of the youth delegates. She spoke both to youth groups and to adult audiences. She designed exhibits for the Council publicity work and has participated in all the sessions of the executive committee. She served on the 1952 nominating committee. Along with this she was an active member of the Future Homemakers of America organization. At the time of this report she has entered college. Though maintaining her interest in the work of the Council her activities have had to be curtailed. Another representative to the Council was the president of the Future Farmers of America. He is always listened to with respect, and

[6] This second idea from Iowa comes from the Iowa City Woman's Club project reported earlier and separately.

his remarks carry weight. One of the youth representatives to the Council wrote that one thing wrong with the White House Conference was "that all the youth were from the right side of the tracks" and that she was proud of the Kansas Council for making sure that all youth was represented.

To illustrate what the young lady means: One of the most active and constructive members of the Council is a young man of Mexican blood. The report of the Council states that "he is not in the upper socio-economic group and is a member of a minority group. Nevertheless he has made a real contribution to the Council."

He spearheaded a survey of the use of marihuana in the Mexican colony here. At the present time (1953) he is serving his turn in the army. Even so his thoughts were with the Council and its work. He began thinking about the possible harm done to young people, in temporary trouble with the law, by having their names published in the newspaper. His first letter writing resulted in a poll of the opinion of Kansas newspapers on the subject to which 95 editors replied. There was majority opinion that names should not be published except for traffic violations and drunken driving. The net result of the thought and action of this one young man has been an increasingly constructive adult approach to the problem of juvenile delinquency. His continuing interest is the result of service as a teen-ager on an adult state council.

The good example set by this Council of including young people among its regular membership has exerted influence beyond the Council itself. "A number of the agency members of the Council now have youth as active members on their adult boards and committees." "A high school PTA has a student as a third vice-president, who with four other young people, one from each class, serve on the Board of Managers." One hundred fifty-four Women's Clubs in Kansas were, in 1953, engaged in community projects which involved full participation and co-operation of youth. One woman wrote, "A highlight of our program was learning that youth are quite responsible and co-operative with adults—when adults work with them."

Mr. Tucker closes his report this way: "Frankly I fear that as adults we have not given enough attention to the potentialities of youth in our planning bodies, even perhaps in our policy groups. In our Council I know we have not utilized youth to the maximum extent. One of our problems has been in being able to obtain representative youth who could arrange time and finances to attend meetings. Another handicap has been the reluctance of some adults to share with youth actual participation in discussions. Too frequently some of our agenda items for our executive committee sessions do not come within the range of experience and information of youth.

"Yet, I am convinced that as a youth process, we on the Council are realizing some vital benefits from this association with youth."

SOMETHING TO FRAME FROM KANSAS

1. *Seek the potentialities of youth regardless of race, creed, color, social or financial status.*
2. *Adults and youth can work together in a single Council.*
3. *Face up to the problems but keep faith in the adult-youth participation principle.*

Report from Michigan

Michigan's Youth Commission was appointed by the Governor in 1949. The chairman is Mrs. Margaret Price who served as chairman of the Council on State and Local Action for the 1950 White House Conference. This was one of the three Advisory Councils for the conference. She is exceptionally active in working for extended adult-youth participation and co-operation throughout the state. We are indebted to Mr. Sam Rabinovitz, the executive secretary of the Commission, for this report.

The core of the report is the organization and work of a very dynamic "Youth Advisory Council." The idea for the Council was sparked by the six Michigan youth delegates to the White House Conference. These young people told the Commission that they wanted a chance to sit down with adults in school, church, community centers and Council of Social Agency meetings to help plan programs and carry their share of responsibility. They requested the Commission to help them in an effort to enlist other youth in such a venture. This the Commission was glad to do.

The organizational meeting took place in May, 1951, with 45 young people representing 25 state-wide organizations present. There was one adult consultant to every three youth delegates. Adults were urged to participate in the discussions but could not interfere or vote in the organizational proceedings.

Unlike most new organizations they did not draw up a constitution but they did state their purpose and formulated the following rules for themselves:

We, the youth of Michigan, are gathered here to assist and advise the Michigan Youth Commission on our problems to the end that we may become better citizens of our state and nation. This would be achieved by:

1. Acting as a sounding board for youth ideas.
2. Securing proportional representation on the Michigan Youth Commission to include high school youth, working youth, as well as college students.
3. Helping obtain a working voice for youth in planning and carrying out programs which affect us all.
4. Promoting legislation for youth."[7]

This was the simple working basis until the end of 1953 when they defined their functions a little more sharply. They decided that YAC, as they called their Council, was primarily educational in relation to organizations represented in the Council and advisory in relation to the Youth Commission; that all

[7] Minutes, Youth Advisory Council, May, 1951.

legislative recommendations should not be directly presented by the Council but should go through the Youth Commission. They recommended that the Youth Commission send a regular delegate to each Council meeting. This was in addition to the adult membership on their Executive and Finance Committees. They also formulated the principle that when voting is recorded, it be clearly understood that opinions expressed by an individual do not commit the delegate's organization.

This last provision indicates a determination that the Council's actions should be truly representative. This principle they were aware of at the outset.

"From the beginning the young people seemed to be unusually aware of the importance of the meaning of 'representation.' They laid great stress on the importance of delegates reporting back to their organizations and that ideas be returned to the Council at the next meeting."[8]

To illustrate this point, in February, 1952, the Council held a two-day meeting at which they stipulated "that members of the Council serve for two years and that one representative be replaced each year by the sponsoring organization." At this same meeting a workshop was organized around the question, "Should 18-year-olds vote?" The Council itself was in favor of it but delayed action until each delegate could consult his organization and report back to the Council. The Council minutes of May 17-18, 1952, include a report by every organization as to (1) how the organization opinion was obtained and (2) the result of the method used to obtain it. At this same meeting also, they worked out plans to find youth representatives of large groups who belong to no organization. They have been reasonably successful in doing this which is at the very point where adult as well as youth "representative" organizations fail.

In January, 1954, a formal constitution was drawn up and ratified in February, 1954—almost three years after the organization began to function. Being aware of the nature of political

[8] Summary of minutes, p. 1, Business Meeting, Michigan Youth Commission Workshop, at which the Youth Council was organized.

structures, they re-affirmed that "regardless of the change in state administration which may affect the Michigan Youth Commission, the Youth Advisory Council shall continue to function." This idea, Mr. Rabinovitz stated, was in their original structure.

An official letter from Mrs. Price, Chairman of the Michigan Youth Commission, in May, 1951, formally invites three members from the Council to become regular, voting members of the Michigan Youth Commission, pending official appointment by the Governor. She suggested that two of these be high school students and one be a working youth since they already had three college students on the Commission. The chairman of the Council was invited to be an ex-officio member. She informed them that all expenses of the young people, serving on the Commission, would be paid. Prompt and favorable action by the Governor followed. With this action in 1951, the State of Michigan officially recognized the principle of adult-youth participation.

With regard to the purpose and structure of the Michigan Youth Advisory Council, three important points should be noted: (1) It was organized as a youth participation program, but for the primary and stated purpose of co-operation with the adult Michigan Youth Commission. There are youth delegates on the Commission and adult delegates on the Advisory Council. This arrangement provides a two-way street as a basis for understanding and joint action. (2) They moved ahead slowly and waited until they had had enough experience before setting up their permanent structure, represented by a formal constitution. (3) They have taken every possible precaution to make sure that all their actions represent the points of view of *all* youth.

So much for the structure—what does this Council do? They hold two-day meetings at least once a year with regular sessions in between. At the first of these the Governor was present. The afternoon was devoted to a sober, realistic consideration of "Youth Responsibility and the Narcotics Problem." Dr. Ralph C. Rabinovitch, Chief of the Children's

Division of the Neuropsychiatric Hospital, University of Michigan, was the discussion leader. He is a nationally recognized authority.

Other subjects which have come up for discussion are The Reorganization of School Districts, in order to assure each young person an adequate education which the districts, at the time, did not allow for; and Equal Opportunity for Employment of Youth. The Council sent a recommended fair employment practice bill to the Youth Commission. After consideration and discussion the Commission forwarded it to the State Legislature. It did not pass the first time, but the Commission and the Council together continued to work for it. The discussion of driver training resulted in a state-wide Driver's Training Conference cosponsored by the Council and the State Safety Council. Their discussions and recommendations concerning Counseling Services for Youth made adults sit up and take notice. They recommended that it be compulsory for each young person to receive Counseling Service every six months and drew up a detailed, practical plan which they submitted to the adult Youth Commission. This created adult interest and support in the following ways: (1) 1500 copies were distributed to a PTA convention; (2) representatives from the Youth Commission and the Youth Advisory Council met with the State Superintendent of Instruction. Through his office, the recommendations were passed on to every principal and counselor in the state; the Michigan Federation of Teachers prepared an article for their magazine; and the Michigan Employment Security Commission sent out a release, under the name of Charlotte Peterson, President of the Council, to sixty-seven branch offices and to all members of the State Staff.[9]

The Council in co-operation with and encouragement of the Michigan Youth Commission is not only taking the initiative but being asked to help. For example, they were asked for

[9] Minutes, Youth Advisory Council, February, 1952, and supplementary material supplied by Mr. Rabinovitz.

ideas on how to integrate youth representatives on the Detroit Mayor's Committee. Mr. Ralph W. Daniel, Director of the State Board on Alcoholism, requested the Council to set up a committee to study the question in relation to youth.[10] The Youth Labor Laws Committee sent the Council a large packet of materials and asked them to design a pamphlet giving accurate and adequate legal employment information for the 14-18-year-old age group.[11]

So, in very broad strokes, this is the story of what six enthusiastic young people—given a taste of adult-youth participation through a large national conference—have been able to do when adults were ready and willing to work with them. Mr. Rabinovitz, himself, said very little. He simply packed up documentary material all classified so that the progress of the Council could be seen. He did say this in his accompanying letter:

"This Youth Advisory Council is by no means a finished product. As a dynamic instrument it will have its ups and downs. Honest mistakes will be made. In fact, the members of the Youth Commission have much to learn about adult-youth participation, but they all have a deep faith in the contribution youth can make in building a better community. They all have a conviction that adults have the responsibility of giving youth the opportunity to do so."

SOMETHING TO FRAME FROM MICHIGAN

1. *No youth group represents youth opinion in a community or state unless all youth, organized or unorganized, have an opportunity to make their ideas known.*

2. *Adults must have abiding faith in youth's ability to do, and conviction of adult responsibility to provide opportunity for youth to do.*

---

[10] Minutes, Youth Advisory Council, Oct. 31 and Nov. 1, 1953.
[11] Minutes, Youth Advisory Council, Feb. 14-15 and May 16-17, 1954.

3. *Adults must provide adequate advisory help and adequate, accurate information for youth both in printed form and through qualified speakers.*

4. *Adults must give full credit to youth for youth's ideas and accomplishments.*

5. *Adults must establish at the beginning, and maintain, adult warmth, cordiality, respect, and a sense of real partnership with youth.*

6. *Miracles won't happen and mistakes will, but youth will grow into responsible citizenship if adults do not let them down.*

Report from Wisconsin

Wisconsin has a Committee on Children and Youth appointed by the Governor in 1948. Members of the already established Madison Youth Council have served on this committee from the beginning. Wisconsin also has a unique committee called the "Youth Committee for Community Participation" which has a state-wide representative youth membership. Miss Mary Denton is the staff adviser to this committee. We are indebted to her for this report and to teen-ager Bob Grady, president of the committee 1953-54, for his comments about its value.

ORIGIN OF THE YOUTH COMMITTEE

The reason for this committee can best be stated by an excerpt from a youth report presented at the Second Governor's Conference on Children and Youth in 1952.

Young people in Wisconsin recognize that they have important rights and responsibilities in their own communities, and many have accepted the challenge to actively participate in community affairs and planning. . . . The Wisconsin delegates to the White House Conference, the Madison Youth Council, and other youth groups were concerned about how they might help youth in the state to take the initiative in meeting their problems in the local community. They recognized that one of the great hurdles was to convince adults that youth could participate in planning their own programs and community affairs which affect them; that youth-adult joint planning and participation was important if youth were to learn how to be active citizens in the community when they leave high school without waiting until they are 25 or 30 years old. . . . Youth are ready to show they are able and willing to work with adults in planning their programs, in working on civic projects and community planning.[12]

The idea for such a committee grew out of youth workshops set up around the subject of youth's responsibility to the community during the first Governor's Conference on Children and Youth held in 1951. About 250 young people participated in this conference with adults. A planning committee was elected to work out plans for a permanent Youth Committee. By April, 1952, the planning committee was ready to report. A three-day conference of youth was called by the planning committee and the Wisconsin Committee on Children and Youth. There were over four hundred teen-agers and one hundred adults in attendance. This conference included a meeting of the executive committee of the Wisconsin Committee on Children and Youth which also has young people in it. The plan for the permanent youth committee was thoroughly discussed at this meeting with the planning committee present. Before the close of the conference, the plan was approved by this committee and by the conference itself. Other work done at the youth conference consisted of workshop discussions of how youth could participate through youth centers, in rural communities, through churches and schools, on organizational boards and adult committees, and through youth councils. Two sessions were devoted to youth councils in relation to their function in participation in community affairs. One workshop spent its entire time in considering what the role of the adult could be in furthering adult-youth participation.

The plan for the Youth Committee called for the division

[12] Report from District III—Wisconsin Youth Committee for Community Participation, August 25, 1952.

of Wisconsin into ten districts corresponding to the ten districts of the State Department of Public Welfare's Division for Children and Youth. The committee was to be composed of four delegates from each district and after the first year two of the four delegates were to be elected each year for a two-year term, with one of the four to be elected chairman for the district. They made sure that the district organization would be identical in purpose with the larger State Youth Committee except that each district should plan at least one youth conference a year, of its own. They provided for a district executive committee made up of the four district delegates to the state committee, one of whom is chairman of the district, and two other district officers. Adult advisers are elected by districts for a term of one year with professional service to the district provided by a district community consultant. This plan provides both stability and continuity in membership and program for the Youth Committee itself and, at the same time, opens up a wider opportunity for young people to serve and participate through the additional district organization plan. Miss Denton says, "As far as I know, this is the only state which has developed a youth committee that is 'on its own.'" This organizational plan had been in operation a year and a half, as of January 1954. Miss Denton gives us a report of how the plan had functioned to that time:

Since the 1952 conference at which the plan was adopted, eight out of ten districts have sponsored district conferences of from 200 to 500 young people. For the most part their workshops were around the subject "How Can We Be Active in Our Communities?" In about a year more than 2,000 boys and girls have come together to talk about and plan for participation in their communities. There has been a growing awareness on the part of adults that youth can assume responsibility. We see it particularly in the growth of youth councils, youth centers, and youth representation on adult boards and committees and on community councils. There is also an increasing awareness on the part of school people of the value of these youth participation programs.

Among the things which the total committee has done are these: cosponsored with adults two institutes on "Better Radio and Television Listening" completely chairing one section of the Institute; served with the Wisconsin Committee on Children and Youth through their ten representatives. They sent their president and vice-president to the 1952 "Two-Year White House Progress Conference" in New York; worked with the Free Library Commission in preparing a reading list on Youth Participation; helped, with adults, to plan the third Governor's Conference and planned a one-day conference of their own which met just previous to the main conference in preparation for their participation in the conference and polled their own youth members on youth interests, which the adult committee members had already done with adults.

The third Governor's Conference on Children and Youth took place in April, 1953. At the one-day youth conference, held the day before the main conference convened, workshops were set up around the subject scheduled to be discussed at the main conference which adults and youth had planned together. These were Law Enforcement, Family Life, Youth and Community Affairs, Human Relations, Youth Employment, and The Military Draft. Each youth group selected one person to present the group's findings to the corresponding adult group of the main conference, and there were twelve youth sections. During the actual program, apart from the workshops the young people participated in this adult conference in the following ways: Two young persons were on a panel with seven adults discussing the question of Youth and Law Enforcement. A panel on "Our Community Team—Are We Really Letting Youth Participate?" was chaired by a young person. The panel itself consisted of three youth and three adults. Four other panels had youth spokesmen on them. The entire program at the Governor's dinner consisted of dramatizing real adult-youth programs being carried on in communities throughout the state. The Governor's Commission on Human Rights had requested that the Youth Committee nominate a youth advisory board to their commission. A group of high school seniors was presented at this conference as the first youth advisory board to a State Agency."

The Districts have been active apart from the youth conferences. They have participated in "Get Out the Vote" campaigns, helped with the distribution of stickers and folders prior to election, have made election posters, and helped mail out campaign literature. They have helped, with adults, to develop adequate recreational facilities and programs and have tackled both teen-age drinking problems and traffic accidents. Many communities, because of the youth activity in the districts, now have youth on their Councils of Social Agencies or Community Councils. The communities have youth on their Councils of Human Relations or Human Rights, and Madison has youth on the Mayor's Committee on Teen-Age Drinking.

Bob Grady, president of the Youth Committee for Community Youth Participation was asked, "Do You Think Adult-Youth Participation Is Doing Any Good?" This was a routine question included in a questionnaire sent to about sixty young people, Bob among them. In answer he says:

> Youth and adults throughout the whole state are meeting together to better their own communities, thus strengthening the state and the nation. They are forming new youth councils, youth centers and youth center boards, community planning groups with both adults and youth. The Governor's Commission on Human Rights now has a Youth Advisory Board.
>
> Youth are being asked by adult boards and even town boards to meet with them on recreational needs. Thus we feel we are being recognized not as the younger generation but as the generation that is sure that tomorrow will be the America we want. . . .
>
> Though I am proud of many things, this sense of achievement that I am doing my bit has filled me to overflowing with a pride in my country and all therein that has never been equaled in my life. Adults and youth are working in perfect harmony whenever each is given an equal chance. . . . We youth like to be recognized as an equal but always look to adults for their advice because we know that their experience has preceded ours—and with them and their experience and our own effort we can have a better America for tomorrow.

When this answer was read we were curious to know whether such ideas came from a well-balanced young man or from one who was superior but more or less of a "lone wolf" even though he was president of the Wisconsin Youth Committee. Such things do happen. We wanted to use his answer but had promised not to quote any teen-ager, directly, without permission. When permission was requested, we asked for a brief biography. Here is the information he sent.

He was elected to the Youth Committee from his district as a sophomore in high school for a two-year term and elected to the presidency of the committee in 1953. He served as program chairman for a youth conference and as a member of the planning committee for a Governor's Conference. He was 17 in March, 1954, and has played a sousaphone in the school band for four years. He was co-manager of his school paper and won second place in an "I Speak for Democracy" contest. He plans to attend the University of Michigan to study architectural engineering and hopes to get into the NROTC. As a footnote to the letter in answer to the request for permission to quote him, he says: "Please excuse the delay in writing, but I have had a busy week end working and trying to get in a little hunting. (Signed) Bob Grady."

SOMETHING TO FRAME FROM WISCONSIN

1. *Organization of youth by state districts is a practical plan for developing widespread youth participation which naturally leads out into adult-youth participation and co-operation in communities and in the state as a whole.*

2. *Youth can plan conferences for themselves, help to plan adult-youth conferences and participate with adults in such conferences.*

3. *Youth can become interested in community affairs and carry responsibility for helping with them.*

4. *Adults and youth can work together wherever they may be, if each is given an equal chance.*

Guideposts from the Midwest States—a Summary

Young people do not want to be left alone and they do seek adult guidance.

Community projects, to be successful, must be adequately guided by adult groups. Youth needs acceptable adult help and accurate information both in printed form and through qualified speakers. An idea for needed action can come either from an adult or a youth group, but a satisfactory solution emerges only when the two age groups plan the action together and carry out the plan together. Establish adult warmth, cordiality, respect, and a sense of real partnership with youth at the beginning of any adult-youth undertaking and maintain it throughout.

Seek the potentialities of youth regardless of race, creed, color, social, or financial status. No youth group "represents" youth opinion in a community unless all youth have an opportunity to make their ideas known. Youth should have full credit for their own ideas and accomplishments. Youth can plan conferences for themselves, help to plan adult-youth conferences, and participate effectively in both kinds. Youth *can* become interested in community affairs and carry responsibility for helping in them. A co-operative adult-youth project can help youth to become experienced and mature enough to go ahead "on their own."

Some kind of organizational structure which, by its nature, makes adult-youth joint action desirable and possible is a practical necessity. The state can and perhaps should provide expert help in community planning and encourage adult citizens to make use of it in relation to the welfare of youth.

Organization of youth by districts, within a state, is a practical plan for developing widespread youth participation which can lead naturally into adult-youth participation and co-operation. Building slowly, gradually, intelligently and thoroughly through adult-youth councils, similarly organized community by community, is another practical method of achieving adult-youth co-operation. Adults and youth can also work together in a single community council.

Adults and youth can work together wherever they are, *if* each is given an equal chance. Face up to the problems created by adult-youth efforts, but maintain faith in youth's ability to do. Let this faith be based upon the conviction that it is adult responsibility to provide youth with the opportunity for constructive and appropriate action. Adhere stoutly to faith in the adult-youth participation principle.

Miracles won't happen and mistakes will, but youth will grow into responsible citizenship, *if* adults do not let them down.

CHAPTER 5 | # HOW SCHOOLS CAN FOSTER ADULT-YOUTH CO-OPERA-TION

Through concrete illustrations we have shown how youth group activity within adult sponsored youth organizations, or within special programs of one kind or another, provides both general and specific kinds of citizenship training. Specific illustrations have indicated also that such training was sufficient to allow many teen-agers to participate effectively in the 1950 White House Conference with adults and that it is still sufficient for increasing activity with adults in communities and in several states.

Some of the illustrations reveal that young people without youth group experience are also capable of working with adults although their opportunity to do so is more difficult to achieve and it takes somewhat longer for their efforts to show results.

Our statistics show that there are some four million teen-age boys and girls who belong to no organized, adult sponsored and guided youth groups, either because of the lack of opportunity to join or because they do not choose to join.

It seems to us that the evidence that teen-agers can benefit from youth group experience and at the same time enjoy it is convincing. There is also strong evidence that such experience is an asset in developing ability to share community responsibility with adults.

The following program opens up the opportunity for every boy and girl in high school to gain the benefits of youth group experience.

IMPROVING CITIZENSHIP EDUCATION PROJECT

This is a service project, supervised by Teachers College, Columbia University, in New York City, and financed by the Carnegie Foundation of New York. It started as an experiment in eight school systems in New York, New Jersey, Connecticut, and Pennsylvania in 1949. By August, 1950, 78 school systems had adopted the program. By the end of 1951, 130 school systems were collaborating. By December, 1954, more than a thousand school systems in over forty states, State Education Departments, teachers' and liberal arts colleges were participating in the program. By December, 1955, the number of school systems and colleges actively collaborating had grown to over twelve hundred.

This report is based on a brochure called "Improving Citizenship Education Project"; an interview with Dr. Willis H. Griffin, head of the Program Development Division of the project; and the file of "Laboratory Practices" made available through the courtesy of Dr. Griffin, who also edited and approved this report. As Dr. Griffin says, "Unless boys and girls get this kind of experience in high school, many of them will never get it at all."

HOW THE PROJECT WORKS

The heart of the program centers in "Laboratory Practices." The laboratory is a specific situation within the school or community calling for study and action. Such a situation is ferreted out by a class in English, Social Studies, or some other specific subject. The group decides whether or not to try to do something about it. The practices have the purpose of developing the skills needed to deal effectively with the chosen situation. Adults (teachers) serve at all times in an advisory capacity. As the "practice" develops, other adults are drawn into the process as "beginning partners" in the enterprise and often as full co-operators. The best way to make the meaning of this potentially dynamic program clear is by illustrations. Three, out of hundreds, have been chosen because when put together they show the complete process by which adult-youth co-operation may be achieved.

Columbia High School, South Orange, New Jersey[1]

A class of Seniors was given a chance to choose books for the school library. A written agreement was drawn up in which the school authorities gave the class the right to set up committees. It further outlined the qualifications which the books must meet, required that certain information be filed before the books were purchased, and stipulated that they could spend $120.

The class with the help of the teacher divided into the four following committees: (1) Charter—which set down the objectives of the "laboratory practice"; (2) Questionnaire—which sounded out student opinion and taste regarding books; (3) Browsing Room—which, with the librarians, made a survey of what students actually read for the purpose of arriving at valid criteria for the eventual choice of books; (4) Taxpayer's Dollar—which got information from other local libraries about library costs, support, and services.

The list of forty-three books, finally made up by all committees working together, met the standards agreed to and also seemed to be what the students wanted. When the books arrived, the class members sponsored a series of early morning school assemblies at which each of the new books was reviewed. Everyone was invited, but attendance was voluntary. The report states that the class whose laboratory practice it was, was surprised by the large attendance.

The faculty thought that the books were a good selection. Teachers and librarians felt that the students developed understanding about a library, its weaknesses, its strength and, above all, its needs. The students said they learned "respect for the opinions and tastes of others"—"respect for the sensible

[1] TH No. 1—Citizenship Education Project.

use of power"—"how to make decisions that will help fellow students as well as yourself."

Webster Groves, Missouri, Spring 1951[2]

A $200,000 swimming pool was closed by the Mayor because a high court ruled that the town's 2,000 Negroes must be able to use the pool unrestricted or on alternate days. The High School Seniors in a "Citizenship Education Project" decided to "practice" citizenship by seeing what they could do about it. Opinions in the class were divided. Some thought complete segregation was the answer, some thought another pool should be built for Negroes, and some thought there should be unrestricted swimming for both races.

THIS IS HOW THEY TACKLED THE PROBLEM

First they selected ten adults to serve as their "Citizens Advisory Committee." They outlined the problems with this committee and then divided themselves into four committees to gather the facts about the problems as outlined with the adult group.

The first committee consulted the head of Washington University Health Service. He is an expert on swimming pool sanitation. He told them that there is no evidence of disease communication when public pools are chlorinated and treated. He also told them that if Negroes were denied the use of the pool because of greater susceptibility to disease due to poor housing, diet, and so on then the "poor" whites would have to be excluded for the same reason.

The second committee investigated and found out that Negro recreational facilities were far below the need. Young Negro people were invited to give their viewpoint. This committee also investigated the financial aspect of the problem through an interview with the mayor. He pointed out that if the pool were opened for mixed swimming, white attendance

2 TH No. 7—Citizenship Education Project.

would drop off and the cost of operation could not be covered. The third committee polled parental attitudes. The fourth committee found out from other towns how they had solved the problem and the results of their chosen solution.

When all the information was in, students made a report at a Rotary Club meeting. This report included a recommendation that the town appoint a Human Rights Commission to study the issue and make a definite recommendation which should be binding. The present (during 1951 when this project took place) indication is that such a commission will be formed.

A lawyer said, "No committee of adults could have done a finer, fairer job." A minister said, "They started with open minds about what might be the best solution to the problem. They dug and dug for facts. Eventually we shall have mixed swimming here and I think the cool, factual report of these young men and women will have been a major factor. But, most of all, they set a good example for their elders, on how a good citizen or a group of them can tackle an explosive situation coolly and calmly."

The boys and girls themselves were enthusiastic about this project. One student expressed the feeling of all when she said, "I learned more from this than from a dozen textbooks." Another youth also expressed the group feeling when he said, "This type of thing deals with real problems instead of artificial ones."

Tacoma, Washington's City Charter[3]

Tacoma's Commissioners were not getting along together and everybody knew it. There was a great deal of confusion. The students in a class in American Government decided to do something about it. This was in the Stadium High School in Tacoma. A Board of Free Holders was to be elected in the spring. One of the jobs to be done then was to write a new

[3] TH No. 2—Citizenship Education Project.

city charter. The students set out to find what kind of charter the people wanted.

They first made up a three-page questionnaire. Then they selected a committee made up of the superintendent of schools, the principal of the high school, an attorney, a housewife, a doctor, a member of the League of Women Voters, a newspaper man, a business man, a minister, and a representative of local clubs. This committee was asked to criticize the questionnaire, on the basis of which the students were to make a survey to determine public opinion about the kind of new charter desired.

On the basis of the final questionnaire agreed upon, after this criticism, each student interviewed ten voters, totaling approximately 330 people, representing a cross section of Tacoma sentiment. They found that practically nobody was satisfied with the present Tacoma government. Only a few people liked the present commission. Tacoma people in general were well informed about their city government, and the majority understood the role that the Board of Freeholders would fill. They found that the new charter hoped for was a city manager system. The students then gave their findings to the committee of citizens who had criticized their questionnaire. Then they publicized their findings through the press, radio, television drama, and recordings.

At the time of this [laboratory] practice, the election had not taken place. But regardless of the outcome, the students themselves profited by finding out how to discover public sentiment and how to mobilize public opinion in a democracy.

The Values of the Citizenship Education Project

The values of this project run in a number of different directions. The first, that of providing organized youth group experience for all teen-agers, provided adults are willing, has already been emphasized.

Beyond this there is the advantage of helping the boys and girls to see from experience that their studies have application to real life situations. This is by no means the least of the values. There is probably no more common complaint among teen-agers than this: "I don't see why I have to study history or government or economics or a lot of this stuff. It isn't any use to me."

In these illustrations economics was involved in the costs of books for the library and the swimming pool as well as tax money and its use. English was involved through the report to the Rotary Club, making sense out of a questionnaire as well as reports presented on radio and television, and through the press. Government took on reality and social studies came to life in tackling a very real and explosive situation which is a problem nationally as well as locally. Thus it can be seen how this program can co-ordinate all the subjects "taken" in school and bring them to life as they are related to effective citizenship in any community within our American republic.

The greatest value of this project[4] is that it provides that kind of youth experience which can and does lead into co-operative relationships with adults in the school and community for all boys and girls in high school. It engenders adult confidence in teen-age abilities among those adults who work with the young people as they complete their "laboratory practice." It allows the young people to find out for themselves how the democratic process functions in real life. The evident satisfaction gained by the boys and girls from being a part of the process in real situations cannot help but lay the foundation for strong faith in our free way of life. This is the basis for good citizenship.

4 "Improving Citizenship Education Project" a brochure, and a small pamphlet called "What You Can Do" available on request from "Improving Citizenship Education Project," Teachers College, Columbia University, New York 27, N. Y.

CHAPTER 6

HOW ADULTS CAN FOSTER ADULT-YOUTH CO-OPERATION

A large-scale canvas has thus far been painted which gives a composite picture of the adult-youth co-operative process. In order to reproduce this large picture on the small canvas of our individual homes, organizations, and communities, we need to look more closely at three details: (1) a personal realization of the importance of listening to youth, (2) preparation of adults and teen-agers for the co-operative process, and (3) opportunities which can set the process in motion. The outline representing the purpose of the process—good citizenship—and the conditions which make the process possible—mutual adult-youth confidence—have the same relative place on the small canvas as on the large.

The Importance of Listening to Youth

Whatever adults try to do in the home, in the school or church, in any organization or community, they must first, last, and always be ready to listen to the teen-agers' point of view, remembering that not all teen-agers have yet learned to be diplomatic and tactful in expressing themselves. Neither have all adults. The listening must be with the same respect as would be shown to one's contemporaries. Adults must be willing to express their point of view on the same subject with dignified respect for themselves and with dignified respect for the teen-ager whose turn it is to listen.

Sophocles expresses the eternal struggle of youth to attain a place of respect on his own merits, and of adults to resist yielding their advantage of years and experience even when the young person has a legitimate and often accurate point of view. He wrote in "Antigone" the following dialogue:

> *Creon:* Men of my age, are we indeed to
> be schooled then, by men of his?
> *Haemon:* In nothing that is not right; but
> if I am young, thou shouldest look
> to my merits, not to my years.[1]

Three comments of modern youth (taken from their own report of their reactions to adult-youth participation during the 1950 White House Conference) are not unlike Haemon's feelings as he responds to his father's question. They said: "An adult is not determined by age but by the degree of maturity he has attained." . . . "We realize that there is a natural barrier between youth and adults created by age and degree of experience. We know that these factors are real but too often they have become exaggerated in the minds of both adults and youth." . . . "In the opinion of youth, some adults act as if young people will always remain rash, incompetent, uninterested, and selfish. If we are made to feel incompetent, we may soon believe that we have no capabilities."[2]

Youth as well as adults have a point of view about the adult-youth co-operative idea and about the kinds of adult attitudes which help or hinder the development of co-operation between the two age groups. In the light of our urgent plea that teen-agers be given a chance to be heard, it would be highly inconsistent if we did not give you an opportunity to listen to their ideas on this subject.

A questionnaire was prepared and sent to each member of Wisconsin's Youth Committee for Community Participation and to about twenty other boys and girls experienced in work-

[1] Sophocles, "Antigone," *A Treasury of the Theatre* (New York: Simon and Schuster, 1940), p. 1600. This quotation was sent to the author by Nick Johnson, a teen-age member of the National Board of a large youth-serving organization.

[2] "Children and Youth at the Midcentury" Report on Youth, pp. 5-6. National Organizations, Federal Government, Midcentury White House Conference on Children and Youth.

ing with adults, making sixty in all. All questionnaires were returned with amazing promptness and each seemed to be thoughtfully and frankly answered.

These are the questions asked of the boys and girls:

1. What are the attitudes of adults whom you find easy to work with?
2. What are the attitudes of adults whom you find hard to work with?
3. Do you like adult-youth participation? Will you try to explain why or why not?
4. Do you think adult-youth participation is doing any good? Can you say why or why not?
5. Are there any other comments you wish to make?

Because all the teen-agers answering the questionnaire have wide opportunity to know what other teen-agers think, the answers to these questions may well be more representative of teen-age ideas than the number of questionnaires sent out would indicate. This would certainly be true of the answers to the first two questions because there are the universal teen-age home situations, apart from the adult-youth relationships through organized joint activity.

To take the last question first, the "other comments" were mostly illustrations of special co-operative projects they were working on. More than half, each in his own unique way said, "Thanks for the chance to say what I think." One girl said, "Parents often lack understanding and are more willing to let someone else lead us, instead of themselves."

All the young people like working with adults. A few comments will indicate the trends of their thinking. A girl said, "Gives me a chance to see the needs of my community and what is being done about them. Gives me a chance to get a closer look at the people who are running the community and the state." A boy said, "We can realize the reason for our adults' ideas by actually working with them. They only seem old-fashioned when we just look on. I find out how and why adults feel as they do." Another boy said, "Gives me a feeling of responsibility. Gradually you learn to work all sides of a question from the side of adults as well as from the side of youth and you can see their reasoning in the matter. Therefore more satisfactory answers to both adults and youth can be worked out." Another teen-ager said, "Wonderful to work with adults who don't consider you just children."

All the answers indicated confidence that adult-youth efforts were doing some good. A number said a simple yes and then added, "but there should be a lot more of it." Several suggested the idea that one teen-ager expressed when he said, "It wouldn't hurt to have more teen-agers on adult planning boards and committees." A girl said, "In some communities yes, and in some no. A lot more young people need to find out that you can have a lot of fun and still do a little work in the community. A certain fraction of youth are the trouble makers but when they see adults and us having fun working together they want to get in on it too. The most important thing is that when adults and youth work together they understand each other better and then they can co-operate." Another girl said, "It is succeeding in breaking down the barriers between youth and adults. Adults are finding that we have some good ideas, and we are finding out that adults are not against us." This idea of improved adult-youth relationships was expressed in one way or another by 95 per cent of these teen-agers who have had a chance to find out what adults are really like. Still another girl said, "Yes, if both adults and youth will compromise and adults will let us make a few mistakes." A 16-year-old boy about summed up what all the teen-agers seemed to feel when he said, "We need everybody and adults always seem glad when they do work with us."

Here is a summary of teen-age opinion about the attitudes of those adults with whom they find it easy to work:

"They are pleasant, co-operative, and sincere; they are willing to allow 50-50 decisions; they are open-minded and enthusiastic; they lack the attitude of 'I know it all' and do not show outmoded prejudice and domination; they can see when we need help, offer it but do not try to force it, demonstrate their confidence in us, and enjoy our successes; they are friendly and nice to everyone; they are willing to admit when they make mistakes and are willing to change their ideas; they are patient, understanding, broadminded, fair and willing to do their share."

Two specific answers to this question seem significant: "The attitude which says, 'I remember when I was young and I can see where your problems are different than mine were because they have a modern slant'—and then leans forward and listens to your problems." And then this one from a boy, "See youth as young adults and not just overgrown children."

With regard to attitudes of those adults whom teen-agers find it hard to work with, the comments were, as should be expected, the exact opposite of those summarized above. Each answer was expressed uniquely, so let's listen to a few of them which seem to be especially significant. This one, for example: "Adults who think it silly to try to 'change things over night' as they put it, but who are not willing to help us change things at all"; or this description, "Unwilling to let us prove our own worth and afraid of too hard work or inconvenience; and when they do condescend to help, things must be done 'my way' or not at all"; and another closely related idea, ". . . those who try to help and then let youth do all the work. We need guidance along the right path, all right, but we need them to help us too and not just sit like a bump on a log"; still another similar one, "Adults who become interested for personal glory and when adult-youth programs become taken for granted, and there is no more glory, they turn to other interests and leave us to sink or swim by ourselves"; a girl said, "Adults who have no children and adults who help only to promote their own child." And finally, this idea which runs as a traceable thread through all their comments on all the questions, "Hardest type of adult to deal with is the one who thinks that we need leaders instead of advisers. We must be guided, for sure, but we must lead ourselves if we are to become responsible citizens."

Listening to youth, then, is the first step which any adult, anywhere, can take toward fostering the adult-youth co-operative process. We have shown that the results of individual action are cumulative. This first step, possible for all adults, can do more to establish an atmosphere of mutual confidence between the two age groups and to improve relationships than any other one effort.

In Preparation for the Co-operative Process

PREPARATION OF ADULTS[3]

Adults can do little about achieving confidence in themselves except by personal contact between themselves and those who have confidence. This is an intimate, personal problem to which each adult must find his own answer.

Older people can, however do something about building adult confidence in youth. They can ensure the community's having an accurate picture of its teen-agers (1) by finding all the facts in relation to teen-age activity in the community both good and bad, and (2) by making sure that these facts are publicized through every medium available.

Such facts can be found through a community survey in which high school boys and girls could help. They are interested in being recognized "as they really are" and, as illustrations have shown, they are capable of getting all the facts on any subject which interests them. They could also help with the publicity. The chances are that teen-agers themselves need a true picture of their activities almost as much as adults do.

What might result from this first step no one can tell in advance. There seems to be little question that it would make the community adults aware that teen-agers do something else besides make noise and dance, if the picture were essentially a good one. If not, it could well lead the adults toward inquiring why the picture was not good and to ask the ques-

---

[3] Helpful booklets available are *How to Lead Discussions* and *Taking Action in the Community* (Adult Education Association, 743 N. Wabash Ave., Chicago 11, Ill.).

tion, "What can be done about it?" The reports of what some communities have already done can help much as suggestions of what can be done and more especially, they provide help in knowing how to do it. This first step might lead into a co-operative project regardless of whether the teen-age picture was good or bad.

PREPARATION OF TEEN-AGERS

The survey conducted primarily for the benefit of adults would be bound to reveal what youth group activities were available in the community and whether they were for all teen-agers or only for some. If they were not for all, three things could be done:

1. Some of the leaders among the young people could meet with some adults for the purpose of discussing the possibility of bringing a youth organization to the community. The teen-agers could be enlisted to find out what the teenage interests are. Organizations could be checked to see which ones were best equipped to meet the teen-age needs. This information is available from almost any public library.

2. Steps could then be taken to see whether the organization could come to the community. Before any adult decision is reached, the teen-agers should know what the possibilities are and share in the decision.

3. Adults could become personally familiar with the "Improving Citizenship Education Project" (see Chapter 5) for the purpose of adequately presenting the idea to the high school PTA, if there is one, and to the school administrators.

Opportunities for Setting the Co-operative Process in Motion

IN THE HOME

The first opportunity is obviously in the home, perhaps so obviously that we tend to overlook the possibility of consciously developing it and the need to do so.

The home is, or should be, the first "bulwark of democracy." It is the place where teen-agers become most intimately acquainted with adult personal and social ideals, either high or low, and with the kinds of attitudes adults can develop toward God, the school, the community, and its social problems whatever they may be, toward our system of government, and toward the world's social and economic problems. Teen-agers are interested in all these things as any experienced adult youth adviser knows. They want to know what their parents think about them and why they feel as they do. They also want to know what parents think about love and marriage, and the kinds of possible work to be done as a way of earning one's living. Those who have been able to develop the kind of permissive atmosphere in the home which allows for free discussion of any subject know that teen-agers are interested.

Pathetically enough, both parents and teen-agers desire a co-operative relationship based on mutual confidence, but too often do not know how to develop it. The most common complaint that youth leaders hear from teen-agers is, "My parents won't let me tell them my point of view," and from parents, "John or Suzie just won't tell me anything." If the desire for mutual confidence did not exist these remarks would not be made either by any teen-agers or any parents. Perhaps one of the best tasks we could undertake would be to try to get the co-operative process going in more homes in our community.

WHAT PARENTS CAN DO

The places where the opportunity exists or can be created are the high school PTA, all the churches, and any type of organization having an adult sponsored youth program for teen-agers.

Many community organizations have parent groups with speakers on family relationships from time to time. Such meetings often do not accomplish much because adults get tired of just listening. Perhaps a different type of program would accomplish more.

A workshop[4] or panel discussion offers excellent opportunities for audience participation. The audience does not get sleepy or bored if it has an active part in a program. There are many films and filmstrips available which emphasize "democracy" in the home. Some come with discussion guides so that a number of participation-type meetings could be planned. One parents' group planned two panel discussions for two consecutive meetings. The subject of one was, "What's good and what's bad about parents." The teen-agers made up the panel, and the audience was composed of both young people and parents. The second meeting had as its subject, "What's good and what's bad about teen-agers." The panel this time was parents, and the audience was mixed but much larger. In both cases the meetings ran overtime because of the flood of questions. The points brought out at each meeting were summarized from stenographic notes, mimeographed, and mailed out to all parents attending the meetings. Reports came in that this type of meeting had done more to help both parents and young people to understand each other than any other program which had been tried. Both age groups profited by "seeing ourselves as others see us." Understanding is the first step toward building mutual confidence.

IN THE SCHOOL THROUGH THE PTA

The reports from the states indicate that PTA's are increasingly finding it a valuable experience for adults and teen-agers alike when youth representatives are included on the PTA board and on special adult committees. They find that the teen-age point of view about the kind of education they are getting is often more valuable than some adult thinking and that it stimulates adult thinking. For example, many boys and girls have expressed the desire for more opportunity to learn about other countries, more world geography, and a wider system of high school exchange students. Perhaps your teen-agers have similar ideas. If they were represented on a

4 A helpful booklet is *So, We Plan a Workshop* (Indiana Council for Children and Youth, 1330 W. Michigan St., Indianapolis, Ind.).

PTA board, adult members could find out and give them an opportunity to express other ideas about how their school could help them more than it does. This is not to say that all their ideas would be practical or that adults should place decisions about their education on the teen-agers. They are not adults and they do not desire to take this kind of responsibility, but they are adult enough to have a right to make suggestions. Adults miss the chance to know what teen-agers think about their school and its opportunities or lack of them unless they are willing to listen.

IN THE CHURCHES

Churches could do much to make their religious education programs more meaningful for teen-agers if they made it possible for boys and girls to share in planning their own programs. The Hi-Y delegates to their Congress expressed the desire to know more about world religions (other than Christianity). Adults have little faith in Christianity if they are afraid to let young people take a look at other influential faiths. Perhaps young people in churches have a desire to consider this aspect of religion and many other aspects not covered by the Sunday School lessons. The only way to find out is to give them an opportunity to think and to discuss with adults.

Minnesota's idea of developing an adult and a youth council could be adapted to a church organization. In the assemblies all matters pertaining to the best interests of the youth in the church could be discussed, and any changes suggested in organization or program could be considered in more detail by a committee of adults and teen-agers. Personal experience with many teen-agers both in the Sunday School and in organized youth groups leads to the conviction that as adults we are falling flat on our faces in meeting the religious needs of our teen-agers and failing to give them an opportunity to express their views. Unless we listen to their religious ideas how can we help them?

IN ADULT SPONSORED YOUTH ORGANIZATIONS

The youth-serving organizations have an unusual opportunity to develop adult-youth co-operative projects. They have a group of young people, sometimes many more than a hundred members who have had the benefit of a thorough-going youth group experience and so are already prepared and waiting for the opportunity to work with adults in the interests of the organization. That they are capable of serving and that they appreciate the opportunity is proved by the fact that those who do have the opportunity want a wider youth representation. And yet, organizational boards and committees, generally speaking, take little advantage of this available supply of potential volunteer members.

For some reason organizations of this type have been slower than community organizations or than communities in experimenting with the adult-youth co-operative idea. For example, it took one chairman of an adult advisory committee three years to persuade the other adults that the teen-agers should be represented on this committee which dealt exclusively with the development of the youth program. Finally two teen-agers were invited to join the committee. At the close of the year the adults thought so well of the idea that plans were made to increase the youth representation.

Adults seem more willing to experiment with youth service on a committee such as we have described than with youth representatives on boards. There are three general schools of thought on this subject. It will be helpful for adult leaders in youth-serving organizations to know about each position because they are almost sure to run into one of them if they suggest including youth on the board of such an organization.

The first group feels that teen-agers should never serve on organizational boards and offers these objections: teen-agers are not of legal age and cannot vote on financial questions; they are inexperienced and therefore can have no voice in policy questions; they are deceived into thinking they have responsibility which they do not have; because adults are in the majority the teen-agers tend to say what adults want to hear; and a teen-age "representative" on a board too often represents only himself.

There are three national organizations having the policy of including teen-agers on their boards. Two teen-agers who had just completed a year's service on each of these boards were asked their opinion about the value of serving on such an adult board. None of them was aware of the point of view expressed above or of the two other points of view we shall present.

The teen-age views with regard to one or two of the points expressed above are these: "A young person would not be qualified to set the salary of an executive but he could have an opinion about his reappointment." Another said, "In all the sessions I felt that I was actually wanted and that my opinions were wanted. Youth today needs to feel wanted." Still another, a boy of 17, said, "A youth has to start getting experience. As far as inexperience goes, many adults are equally unqualified for their responsibilities. When adults are new on boards they have to learn too."

A second group feels this way about teen-age service on boards: good citizenship includes knowledge and support of social agencies in the community as well as civic responsibilities; citizenship is a growth process and teen-agers who are prepared for large experience cannot grow if they do not have opportunity to get it; service with adults on organizational boards and committees is one such opportunity.

For one of the young people, experience on an adult board was a learning experience. He said, "I have gained some knowledge of organizational methods and interrelationships. My own point of view has changed for the better in many ways."

The third group feels that teen-agers should serve on adult boards but with certain limitations which are understood by adults and teen-agers alike. These limitations are "passing on budgets, hiring of staff, setting of professional standards of operation for groups from which they come, and setting of health and welfare standards as they affect the group from which they come."[5]

Another youth opinion on this question is this: "Just as you do not select adult members to boards at random, neither should young people be selected that way. Both should be selected on the basis of individual qualifications. In a sense young people are 'expert' in a particular field arising from our familiarity with the problems of ourselves and our age group. Adults need this kind of information."

IN COMMUNITIES

Each community is unique. What you can do and where you can start no one can say. Five types of possible co-operative adult-youth community activity have been illustrated. The best we can do now by way of suggestion about what can be done is to give the list of known teen-age interests in community activity. All these have shown up in the illustrations which have been used and in many more for which we had no space. The interests are listed in order of the frequency with which they showed up. They are as follows:

1. Improving recreational facilities for themselves and younger children.
2. Service in social agencies on a mature responsibility basis.
3. Community "cleanup-fixup" projects.
4. Development of a teen-age employment program.
5. Traffic problems, including bicycles as well as cars.
6. Civic affairs such as getting out the vote, stuffing campaign envelopes, distributing campaign literature, consideration of laws affecting teen-agers and making recommendations to adult groups for changes in the laws.
7. Dealing with the youth vandalism problem.
8. Collecting and classifying data in relation to youth or other community surveys and composing information booklets for the use of other youth when requested by adults.

[5] Charles S. Levy, *The Group*, 1954.

9. Service on adult boards and committees of organizations having a youth program or having an interest in youth.
10. Participating in adult-youth conferences on youth interests on both the community and the state level.

The interest in the adult-youth conference idea might have been higher up on the list if more young people had had the chance to find out what it was like. This kind of opportunity showed up only in the reports of the five state-wide programs and in the report from Los Angeles. It is listed because of the enthusiasm felt by the young people who had firsthand experience with it.

We should like to suggest one method of setting the co-operative process going in any community. This is the exploratory method which was used with such effectiveness in Clarkston, Washington, and in Fulton, Mississippi. Each community had a slightly different way of going about it, and adults in other communities may also find still different ways. But to explore the possibility is the simplest, most direct way to find a "first" thing to do. And many needs or interests will be discovered in such exploration, some of which may well lead into projects of lasting value to a community.

Summary of Guiding Principles for Adult-Youth Relationships

1. Adults need not be discouraged if progress in developing co-operative group relationships seems slow, for it is the nature of the process itself to move step by step. The slowness is an essential part of the democratic process, which consists of sharing ideas and arriving at a consensus about any contemplated course of action. This takes time. A dictatorship, on the other hand, does not need time, for it says do—and we DO.
2. Mutual confidence, based on adults' confidence in themselves and in teen-agers is inherent in the co-operative process.

3. Opportunity to establish mutual confidence is necessary. Such opportunity is always present wherever adults and teen-agers are. Teen-agers need to have a chance to establish confidence in themselves in order to meet adults with assurance reasonably comparable to that of the grown-ups. Adults must often offer such opportunity to boys and girls. They cannot always find it alone, even though they may desire to do so.

4. Teen-age interest in a subject of conversation or in any situation involving them is a direct invitation to adults to show their interest. In any problem situation in the home or community, adults need to let them go ahead "on their own" toward a solution but assure them of their interest, desire, and willingness to help. Interest constitutes readiness to learn and to learn to do for either adults or teen-agers.

5. Adults must accept each teen-ager "as he is" and look for his potentialities in all respects. Teen-age ability, actual and potential, is not restricted to any special race, creed, color, social standing or financial status.

6. The honest desire of adults to show a co-operative attitude in any situation involving teen-agers and-or other adults is the first requisite for being able to co-operate. Such sincere desire opens the mind to possibilities for co-operative thinking and action to which adults may otherwise be blind (the exploratory method in a community accomplishes this, whether or not a problem exists).

7. First, last, and always, adults must remember that attitudes between themselves and teen-agers, between teen-agers and teen-agers, and between adults and adults are contagious in any individual or group relationship. Listening to the teen-ager's point of view is not a passive but a creative effort to establish mutual confidence and to set the co-operative process in motion toward the goal of becoming partners with youth.

CHAPTER 7

MISTAKES TO AVOID IN CO-OPERATIVE PROJECTS

During the years that the adult-youth co-operative process has been growing, those most intimately associated with the experiments have formulated some dependable and workable guiding principles. Their experience has also made them aware of some mistakes which have been made and should not be made again.

Nine Dangers

As adults start to experiment in their organizations and in their communities it is valuable to know what these mistakes are so that they may be avoided.

1. *Failure to Recognize That a Teen-Ager's First Job is Going to School*

Boys and girls are capable of tremendous enthusiasm. They can be carried away by a challenging project, and it may actually have more appeal to them than some of their studies. It sometimes happens that they put more time on the project than they should, and their school work suffers as a result. Adults must be sure that this does not happen. The Junior Achievement Program recognizes this danger and consciously avoids it.

2. *Failure to Size Up Accurately the Precocious Boy or Girl*

Adults sometimes can be deceived about the reason for the interest of a teen-ager to work enthusiastically with them and so they may uncritically accept such a boy or girl as a representative of a larger group of teen-agers. They need to make sure that the bright responsive boy or girl has made a satisfactory adjustment within his own age group and that he is not seeking adult company merely as a substitute for leadership in his own group, which may have been denied him by his associates.

There are many young people who are genuinely ahead of their age group and yet adjusted to it. They are ready, before the others, for more mature experience and responsibility. Such opportunity should not be denied them. Adults should, however, make very sure that such a boy or girl really represents other groups of teen-agers. If he does not, they may be deceived into agreeing to plans suggested by him which will not at all meet with the approval of the rest of his group or adequately solve some general teen-age problems. Adults can accept such a boy or girl on his own merits as offering a *personal* point of view which can easily be very constructive and helpful when representation is not the important issue in a question being considered. Such experience will help him to mature further.

3. *Cheating the Quiet, Unobtrusive Boy or Girl of Valuable Adult-Youth Experience*

Sometimes an inarticulate boy or girl is more mature than a more vocal young person but he may easily be overlooked. Often such a young person needs only a gentle drawing out in order to discover that he has a real contribution to make. Cheating such a boy or girl of valuable experience is most often apt to happen when adults in organizations are asked to suggest the names of young people who might be interested in an adult-youth program.

4. *Enlisting Teen-Agers in Adult-Youth Projects of Too Wide a Scope*

Occasionally adults include teen-agers in a situation where the topics for discussion and action to be taken are beyond their knowledge and experience without letting them know in advance that they are being offered the opportunity to learn in some respects and to share in other respects. At such times many teen-agers get the idea that "adults say they want us to help but they don't really." This idea which the invited teen-ager may have had will simply be confirmed and will hinder mutual confidence, unless the adults are candid enough to state whatever limitations must be placed upon his participation in the proceedings and the teen-ager is willing to accept the limitations because they are reasonable.

This kind of situation is most apt to be in relation to some organizational adults board or committee whose business is partially but not exclusively youth interests and problems.

5. *Failure to Recognize Teen-Age Maturity and Readiness for More Mature Experience*

To fail to connect teen-age interest based upon readiness and maturity with a chance for more mature responsibility at the very time when he is at a high point of ability to learn, is unfortunate, for once this point is passed, it never comes in quite the same degree again.

6. *Lack of Knowledge of Teen-Age Psychology*[1]

When a group of lay people decide to include some teen-agers in their group or on a committee, it would be a wise procedure to ask some professionally trained person, experienced in youth work, to meet with the adults before inviting the teen-agers. Such a person can be of great help in indicating ways in which the adult group can make the teen-agers feel at home. It is sometimes disastrous to the cause of adult-youth participation if the basic psychology of teen-agers is not understood by the adult majority in the group. Teen-agers want to be understood, but in a natural kind of way. They do not like to have it obvious that adults are trying to understand them psychologically. They want to be understood and accepted as people. To follow this suggested procedure could help to make a first adult-youth meeting a natural, friendly

1 Helpful books available are *On Call for Youth,* Rudolph Wittenberg (Association Press, 1955) and *Leadership of Teen-Age Groups,* Dorothy M. Roberts (Association Press, 1950).

kind. Sometimes a professional person can sit in the group and take the leadership in drawing the teen-agers into the adult discussion. This would help to create an atmosphere conducive to establishing mutual confidence without which co-operation is impossible.

7. *Failure to Be Willing to Admit That Teen-Agers can Sometimes Take the Leadership of Some Phase of an Adult-Youth Undertaking*

When adults and youth are planning a youth program or some special event, the adults may forget that teen-agers are perfectly capable of assuming leadership at certain points. The teen-agers usually know more about what the other teen-agers will or won't respond to, than adults do. To yield the leadership does not mean that the adult withholds his opinions. It is simply an honest adult admission that teen-agers are "experts" in relation to their own age groups. Adults should sometimes listen as well as talk.

8. *Failure to Define What Kinds of Activities Are Suitable for Real Teen-Age Contribution*

On the basis of the present experience of adult-youth co-operative possibilities this failure can be avoided by using the list of situations which have appealed to teen-agers and about which they have proved themselves capable of doing something constructive. This list is in Chapter 6, page 167.

9. *The Temptation to EXPLOIT Teen-Agers*

This is the most serious danger of all. Adults can appeal to teen-agers in such a way as to convince them that the adult cause is their own. The natural ability of this age group to become enthusiastic over something which seems to have value, their eagerness to do something about it, and their lack of experience of adult thinking and ways makes them an easy prey for adults with an axe to grind. The Communists enlist youth just this way; so did the Nazis. Unfortunately other groups sometimes do too. Adults must be alert at all times, but not unduly suspicious. As they work with teen-agers co-operatively they must also be ready to guard them with their own integrity of spirit, against ways of those adults whose motives are not honorable.

Conclusion

We have shown that adult confidence in any teen-ager or in a group of them, which they can feel is genuine, produces a corresponding confidence in us. Relationships improve and mutual confidence comes. When mutual confidence is achieved co-operative activity, with a partnership feeling, becomes both possible and actual. Adults and teen-agers benefit.

When such co-operation is practiced in any type of society the co-operative spirit spreads slowly and gradually to other teen-agers and to other adults, and the community benefits.

Co-operation is a process. It is essentially the democratic process by which our country has grown strong. It is diametrically opposed to dictatorship in any form.

To demonstrate to teen-agers that our faith in this process is strong enough to practice it in all our relationships with them is to transmit that faith to them, in a dynamic way. It is to help them appreciate the freedom which it brings. It is to help them experience the meaning and joy of shared responsibility. It is to provide them with a reason, gained from experience, for defending their developing faith in freedom and trustworthiness as a satisfying way of life.

To make youth aware of our faith in the democratic process is our adult responsibility. Within the framework of the ideals and form of government of our American Republic, we must decide, individually, whether or not we will try to be fully accountable guides and to become partners with the youthful citizens within our sphere of influence. Our attitudes and actions may speak decisively to the young people either for or against the preservation and extension of freedom in the world now and for the years to come.